CHURCH CAFÉS

EXPLORED & CELEBRATED

ROBERT DAVIES

GW00701923

CHURCH IN THE MARKET PLACE
PUBLICATIONS
BUXTON
2002

British Library Cataloguing in Publication Data

A record for this book is available from the British Library

ISBN 1 899147 08 X

CHURCH IN THE MARKET PLACE
PUBLICATIONS
BUXTON

Typeset by
Patricia Saunders, Godmanchester

Cover design by Claire Liversidge

Printed in Great Britain by
Watkiss Studios Ltd, Biggleswade

To all who staff and support
church cafés

Contents

Foreword

by REVD KENNETH STREET, MA
Former General Secretary of the
Methodist Church Property Department

We are much in the debt of Bob Davies for the imaginative titles in the 'Church in the Market Place' series of publications. He has an eye for spotting what others overlook. Here are books of poetry, reminiscences of wartime experiences, as well as reflections on the role of the Church in prison ministry, and more.

The authors and sources are as varied as the titles. From shepherds in the Peak District to a Methodist Superintendent in a city, and a host of 'ordinary folk' who told their tale to be recorded under Bob's editorship.

This present book continues that fine work.

Those whose experience of the Church comes mainly from weddings and funerals or a Christmas Carol Service will be surprised – perhaps shocked – to find that Christian communities up and down the land have a much wider and down-to-earth understanding of their work. Who would have thought that across the country there are so many churches involved in such mundane activities as serving coffee and making sandwiches for their neighbours!

But why do they do it? It is Bob's analysis of the reasons why there is the 'Church in the Coffee Shop', which makes this book so valuable. The gazetteer of places and people makes fascinating reading as we follow in his footsteps during his sabbatical, but these pages are not only about 'who, where and when', but tell us 'why' as well.

We learn that what appears to be a most modern medium (Expresso Christianity?) has its roots within the ministry of Jesus. We are drawn away from our fascination with ritual hymns and prayers, to find our kinship with the carpenter who broke bread upon the hillside for his neighbours.

I particularly enjoyed the comments on the names given to the church cafés. So often we think that the only evangelism which will work is the 'up-front-and-in-your-face' kind where nothing is left to doubt and it is a question of 'take it or leave it'.

The astute Christian managers of these coffee shops tune in to another part of our human psyche – our delight in puzzles and clues and our satisfaction when we find solutions and answers. So here are odd names, which make the visitor ask, 'Why ever is it called that?' From that query, they may be led to discover ... but I say no more – read it for yourself!

This 'hidden message' also has its roots in the ministry of Jesus. Despite the artists of later years, Our Lord had no halo to make himself immediately identifiable as divine. One of his favourite titles for himself was the ambiguous 'Son of man', which could mean anything or nothing. He kept his secret rather like the servant who turns out to be someone else altogether and washes the feet of his friend. So in the coffee shop Christians simply serve, but who knows what others will see?

Of course, this book is far more than an academic and theological exercise, more than a descriptive review of the Church's eating houses, and it is certainly not a Michelin Guide giving stars for the quality of the catering!

It arises out of the deep concerns of Bob's own ministry and that of the congregation at the Market Place Methodist Church in Buxton. During the past twenty years (for fifteen of which Bob has been their minister) this church has completely rebuilt its premises and refashioned them to be an Open House for the people of Buxton. Market Place knows out of its own experience the value of the ministry of the coffee shop and practises what is preached (if that is the right word) in the pages of this book.

In a very small way I was privileged to share in that process – which is why Bob asked me to write this Foreword – because for the years 1985-2000 the Methodist Conference stationed me at our national Property Office based in Manchester where for most of that time I headed up the team there. We were responsible for many mundane matters, the bricks and mortar of the 6,500 chapels and 2,000 houses, which the Methodist Church uses. Purchases, sales, listed building law (indeed all legal matters affecting property), as well as sourcing grant aid for thirty million pounds worth of building work, which local churches carry out each year. The Buxton Circuit kept us busy throughout that period as the members carried out an extensive renewal of its presence in the town and its surrounding villages.

My personal role in this was not as amateur lawyer, architect or surveyor - we had those professionals within the office - but as a minister seeking to discern how property is to be best used for the purposes of the Church. Some people think that the purpose of the Church is to maintain the property, but really it is the other way round!

At this point many people get bewildered, especially good Christians. They say: 'We thought our task was to keep the chapel open and in good repair!' But there's no point in keeping it open simply as a building, or a historically interesting oddity - which is what some listed buildings are.

Our church buildings are only useful if they express - 'body-forth' - what the Church (the people of God) is all about. Put simply (as Someone else put it), that means loving God, loving our neighbour and sharing the Good News. Much of my time in Manchester was spent trying to nudge the ship of the Church in the direction of using our buildings for these purposes. That meant that local churches had to get to know their neighbours, discover their needs and try to meet them. Often that meant not a series of theological lectures, but the modern equivalent of the foot washing, or the feeding of the five thousand.

Which brings us back to the coffee shop. Enjoy it and may you in your local church find your way of using your buildings to love your neighbours.

Acknowledgements

Public Theology for Changing Times by John Atherton, SPCK 2000. John Atherton is Canon Theologian of Manchester Cathedral and Honorary Lecturer in the Departments of Religions and Theology in the University of Manchester. The book was a good sabbatical companion and provided a sound theological framework for this research. Canon Atherton gave permission for the quotations from his book to be included in the text.

Whatever Name or Creed by Andrew Pratt is published by Stainer & Bell Limited, P O Box 110, Victoria House, 23 Gruneisen Road, London, N3 1DZ. This new collection of hymns and songs includes, 'It makes a banquet ...' which was specially commissioned for this book.

The verses from Fred Pratt Green's hymn are also the copyright of Stainer & Bell, who published in 2001 *Serving God and God's Creatures*, a memorial volume to celebrate the life of Frederick Pratt Green.

Methodism and the Love Feast by Frank Baker was published by the Epworth Press in 1957.

'Chester Pilgrim' © Chester Cathedral: www.chestercathedral.com

The sources of other quotations have been acknowledged in the text. It is hoped that no copyright restrictions have been infringed by reproducing illustrations from the publicity material supplied by numerous cafés.

Introduction

How did it all begin?
Methodist Ministers are given three months sabbatical leave approximately every seven years. This is a fairly recent innovation and an opportunity to switch off and do something different. The word comes from the same root as Sabbath which means 'stop doing what you normally do'. During my first sabbatical in 1993, I reflected on eighteen years of prison ministry and wrote a book called *Out of Prison* – still available at £4! Another sabbatical was planned for April to July 2001. Several projects presented themselves as worthy of research, but the penny dropped when in April 2000 I was on my way to a football match in Chesterfield with my son Peter. (We are not supporters of the Spireites – it was an away game for Wrexham who constantly need our support and prayers!) As we passed Cornerstone Café at Chesterfield Central Methodist Church in Saltergate, Peter said, 'Dad, that's what you should do in your sabbatical, something down to earth, research into church cafés. They're usually twice as nice and half the price.'

This rang bells because the café in our church in the Market Place of Buxton has operated for over thirty years on market days and has provided me with contacts I otherwise would never have had. At Hollinsclough, a village chapel in the Buxton Methodist circuit, but tucked away in the Staffordshire moorlands, a café offering hospitality to walkers in the area at weekends was opened when the new hall was built in 1992. To open a café on the Fairfield Estate, a mile out of Buxton town centre, was part of our vision when we pioneered the Faith in Fairfield project in 1998. It all seemed to click – cafés it must be.

How was I to discover where church-based cafés are? It soon became apparent that this sort of information is not generally held

1

at denominational headquarters, although the Board for Mission of the United Reformed Church came nearest to supplying names and addresses very quickly. At a later stage some Church leaders were very helpful. The *Methodist Recorder* and the *Church Times* gave me a few lines announcing that I was researching the origins and development of church-based cafés throughout the country and inviting readers to write to me if they had a café to recommend. This led to over fifty contacts being made and I am grateful to those who responded and put me in touch with a rich variety of cafés. Having had no success with *Life and Work*, the magazine of the Church of Scotland, some friends from North the Border suggested I try the *Sunday Post*. My note appeared in the 'Snippets' column and met with some response, including this letter from Edinburgh:

> During 'The War' my mother helped in a church-run organisation, either C-of-S or inter-denominational, called the 'Huts and Canteens' in Edinburgh. This was to provide meals etc. for members of the forces during transit or leave etc. She was talking about this to our then minister who told us the following story:
>
>> A senior clergyman (possibly a Moderator) was touring the venues with a General, who patronizingly described them as nothing but glorified NAFFIs. (How does one spell that?) He was immediately given the following reply, 'Aye, but it's the glorified that makes the difference!!!'
>
> What a great ecclesiastical put-down.

Information continued to filter through, not only from café organisers, but also from individuals who were only too pleased to recommend a café they had visited. One very helpful correspondent introduced me to six cafés she has known at different stages of her life:

> My first encounter with a Christian café was at the end of the 70s beside Victoria Coach Station in London. **The Well** was run by the

Anglican Church in Eaton Square and was used a lot by travellers as well as office workers nearby. Good wholesome food, lovely staff and atmosphere, religious literature all over the place, but no one hassling you to become a Christian.

My second encounter with a Christian café was in the early 1980s in Richmond, Surrey. A really 'upmarket restaurant' next to the parish church – Richmond being named still as 'one of London's villages'. A lot of famous people live there especially from the acting profession. I didn't get the impression that this was to 'spread the gospel' so much as to 'make money for the church'. Food was superb – very much home-made, but a classier clientele because of its surroundings. It compiled and sold its own recipe books – two very good ones.

My third encounter was with a Christian café in the basement of an office block in Southampton Row very near Holborn Station. Very simple good food. Young enthusiastic Christian staff. Tracts and leaflets around, but no pressure put on anyone to become a follower. However, everyone was willing to be involved in discussion or debate if asked.

My fourth encounter was with **The Olive Branch**, Rhiwbina, Cardiff, run by the Baptist Church there. Simple fayre in the sense that whoever is on duty produces their favourite recipes apart from sandwiches and jacket potatoes. Christian literature around – also a Christian bookshop.

My fifth encounter was with **The Oasis**, Community Church, Abertridwr. This opened late in the 90s with considerable enthusiasm and served hot meals to begin with, but then found that it could not maintain its level of volunteers and so had to concentrate on 'cold buffet / sandwich menu' only. There were a couple of literature and card stands in the entrance of this old house next to the Community Church. This project seemed to me to be more of a 'social service' and amenity than seeking disciples, although I dare say that was what the worshippers hoped for as well.

My final and present encounter is with **The Rock**, Christian

Resource Centre opened in Bedwas. A jaded corner property with great potential became available and the local Baptist Church set up a trust fund to buy the property and to convert it. One bereaved parishioner did put in a large sum of money, and somehow through constant prayer and fund-raising they achieved their financial target to get the place up and running. It has been a resounding success because it has lots of customers, Christian and otherwise. Teachers use it; office workers use it, but more than that it has become a focal point for six denominations in this area who also use it for the Council of Churches meeting.

In a past life, I have worked with a Christian Organisation (Centrepoint in Soho) and have heard people pass the opinion that all these extraneous matters are *not* what the Church is supposed to be about. We are using up Christian energy the wrong way. *I have to disagree.* As followers of Jesus Christ we are supposed to be out there in the marketplace showing what *we* are made of. Something may brush off on to others – not as often as we would like – but we cannot sit in our churches saying 'come on in' because people not brought up to go to church see it as some sort of fearsome walk through our big doors. We have to adopt a different approach.

I compiled a questionnaire to be sent out to all cafés who expressed interest, outlining some basic questions:

- What is the name and address of your church coffee shop/café?
- How long has it operated?
- Why was it started?
- When is it open?
- What food/drink is served?
- How many people are involved in the organisation as paid staff and/or volunteers?
- How many people visit it in a typical day/week?
- Why do people like it?
- What benefits has it brought to your church?

- How would you say the café has contributed to:
  - Fellowship?
  - Evangelism?
  - Community?
  - Fund-raising?

Even though many questionnaires were not returned, I certainly received more than the twenty per cent return that can be expected. I have attempted to include some information in the different sections of the book from each questionnaire returned to me. As with funerals, where there is more to say about some people than others, so with cafés. The uniqueness of the individual goes beyond the length of the eulogy and the significance of a café in any community must not be judged by the amount of space given to it in this book. Where small is beautiful, brief is better, but in order to explore those cafés working on a large canvas and sometimes in collaboration with other projects a proliferation of words becomes inevitable.

On a Sunday morning in June 2000 I informed my congregation in Buxton of what I intended to do and invited them to buy the book, so encouraging me – or forcing me – to write it. It so happened that, unknown to me, two visitors were present from Berkhamsted who have links with one of the largest enterprises featured in this book. They signed up and so confirmed that it must be done. By the time my sabbatical arrived I knew that in order to sample a variety of cafés, I must travel in certain directions. I received from one person 'good wishes for your gastronomical sabbatical' and set out on my journey aware that links must be made with Bible, hymn book, bread, wine and with the ministry of hospitality.

Will it do?
In those now far-off days when every parish had a vicar and most vicars a curate, it was understood that before preaching a sermon the curate would show it to the vicar. One such curate is supposed to have asked, 'Will it do?' to which the Vicar replied, 'Do what?' I am bound to ask the same questions of this book. So here are my hopes:

1. That it will provide a glimpse of the way churches are imaginatively using their resources of people and premises to engage with the community. Let not the words OUTREACH, BRIDGE, WELCOME, FRIENDLY anaesthetise the reader who scrutinises the small print in the Directory. Whilst they are repetitive they spring from the heart of those who carefully completed the questionnaires and who knew not that others were penning the same words to describe their cafés.

2. That it will be a travellers' companion, particularly for those who are connoisseurs of church cafés but previously have only stumbled across them by accident. On a long journey, it could be possible to plan the route stopping at more than one café.

3. That it will create an informal network between cafés. As volunteers in one place set out to fulfil their duties on the rota they may reflect on the fellowship of active service which links them with people they may never meet who are part of the same team.

4. That it will reveal the Christian presence within communities wearing the apron of humility and service. Fred Pratt Green, whose hymnody brings a new dimension to worship, expresses this superbly in these lines :

> Then let the servant Church arise,
> A caring Church that longs to be
> A partner in Christ's sacrifice,
> And clothed in Christ's humanity.

> We have no mission but to serve
> In full obedience to our Lord:
> To care for all, without reserve,
> And spread his liberating Word.

FRED PRATT GREEN (1903–2000)
Reprinted by permission of Stainer & Bell Ltd

A church privileged to be 'a partner in Christ's sacrifice' will not be afraid to enter into partnership with other neighbourhood groups whose motives signal gospel values at work.

> Involvement in partnership itself now becomes part of the Christian task and discipleship. Since the Church is no longer the centre of life, particularly in western societies, its vocation is not to respond by retreating into inward-looking congregationally based churches, but is about taking part with others in promoting better localities.
>
> – JOHN ATHERTON, *Public Theology for Changing Times*

If this book sometimes strays beyond cafés to allied projects, it is in order to emphasise John Atherton's point.

The author, Fay Weldon, said recently in an interview: 'If you think too much about it, the book will never be finished.' This project has taken long enough and I wish to thank all those who, in many different ways, have helped me complete the task.

What is offered here is just for starters.

ROBERT DAVIES
Buxton, 2002

Refreshment

The word refreshment, used sparingly but effectively in the translation of certain biblical texts, is closely associated with cafés. It can also fittingly describe a vital ministry of the Church, which in different ways seeks to renew, invigorate and revive.

Genesis chapter 18 contains the lovely picture of Abraham welcoming strangers to his tent under the Oaks of Mamre:

> Let a little water be brought, and wash your feet, and rest yourselves under the tree. Let me bring a little bread that you may refresh yourselves.

St Paul on his travels often gives thanks for those 'who have refreshed my spirit'. He would certainly have in mind Lydia at Philippi and her spontaneous offer of hospitality to himself and his companions: 'Come and stay at my home' (Acts 16.15).

In the history of the Christian Church there have always been those who have taken seriously two New Testament texts:

> Contribute to the needs of God's people and practise hospitality.
> - Romans 12.13

> Do not neglect to show hospitality to strangers. There are some who, by so doing, have entertained angels without knowing it.
> - Hebrews 13.2

A reminder of this came to me when I read an article about Chester Pilgrim Ale and I followed it up by contacting the Cathedral Administrator, David Burrows, who was quick to supply me with more information:

> In Chester, almost 1,000 years ago, there was a monastery built that

today is the Cathedral. Throughout the ages, its unique heritage and tradition for outstanding hospitality has made it an important place of pilgrimage. In present times, each year, around one million visitors, modern day pilgrims, come to Chester Cathedral to see the most complete medieval monastic complex in the country and discover its haunting beauty. During monastic times, the Benedictine Monks brewed their own beer for themselves, the people of Chester and to refresh the many thousands of pilgrims. Now this fine refreshing ale celebrates that glorious past and through your purchase we are able to raise funds to maintain this beautiful place.

That was one aspect of monastic hospitality and refreshment. Another is clearly seen in *The Rule of St Benedict*. He was born in Nursia at the end of the fifth century, educated in Rome and eventually settled at Monte Cassino where he founded his monastery. The Benedictine rule number 53 relates to the reception of guests:

> Every stranger who comes is to be received as if he were Christ himself, for he says, 'I was a stranger, and you took me in.' When a stranger is announced, let the Prior or one of the brethren go to meet him and receive him with every sign of love. First let them pray together, then let them join in the kiss of peace. To all guests who come or go, the head must be lowered or the whole body prostrated, and Christ adored in their persons for it is Christ who is received. All guests who are received are to be brought to prayers. The divine law is to be read in the guests' presence that they may be edified.

The gospels contain many references to Jesus eating, drinking, sharing meals and table fellowship, often with those whom the religious leaders of the day considered to be undesirable. This earned him the name, 'Friend of sinners'. From Luke chapter 5 we gather that Levi had a conversion party:

> Then Levi gave a great banquet for Him in his house; and there was a large crowd of tax collectors and others sitting at the table with them.   – Luke 5.29

Levi unashamedly invites his friends of long standing to meet his new friend, Jesus. Levi, of course, was one of many who played host to Jesus at meal times. The welcome offered to Jesus at the home of Mary, Martha and Lazarus at Bethany was always a sweet oasis of refreshment. When he himself was host at the Passover meal which became the Last Supper it was in a room provided by an anonymous friend and careful preparations were made.

> When he came to supper with his friends, Jesus took bread, gave thanks, broke it, and gave it to his disciples, saying, 'Take this and eat it. This is my body given for you. Do this in remembrance of me.' In the same way, after supper, he took the cup, gave thanks, and gave it to them, saying, 'Drink from it all of you. This is my blood of the new covenant, poured out for you and for many, for the forgiveness of sins. Do this, whenever you drink it, in remembrance of me.'

'Was ever another command so obeyed?' asked Dom Gregory Dix in his book, *The Shape of the Liturgy*, and then answered his own question by listing some of the circumstances in which people have done this in response to those words of Jesus. He concludes: 'One could fill many pages with the reasons why people have done this and not tell a hundredth part of them.'

Many different names have arisen to describe this meal, because no one name can do justice to the immensity of its significance for those whom it brings into the real presence of the one who said, 'Come to me all who are labouring and burdened and I will refresh you' (Matthew 11.28, Dr Moffatt's translation). By whatever name it is called in different traditions of the Christian Church, what Jesus did and what Christians re-enact involves the sharing of bread and wine.

11

EUCHARIST (thanksgiving) celebrates the life, death and resurrection of Jesus and his continuing presence with us. Thanksgiving is closely linked with offering; and the actions of Jesus at the Last Supper – Taking, Thanking, Breaking, Sharing – celebrate our lives when taken with gratitude, broken and shared. This offertory acclamation often used in modern liturgies is eucharistic:

Blessed are you, Lord, God of all creation.
Through your goodness we have this bread to offer,
Which earth has given and human hands have made.
It will become for us the bread of life.
Blessed be God forever.

Blessed are you, Lord, God of all creation.
Through your goodness we have this wine to offer,
Fruit of the vine and the work of human hands.
It will become for us the cup of salvation.
Blessed be God forever.

Blessed are you, Lord, God of all creation.
Through your goodness we have ourselves to offer,
Fruit of the womb, and formed by your love.
We will become your people for the world.
Blessed be God forever.

By offering bread and wine, work of human hands and fruit of the earth, we receive Christ in turn. So the Eucharist exemplifies the partnership between God and ourselves for our sustenance and the transformation of the world.
    – JOHN ATHERTON, *Public Theology for Changing Times*

MASS (from the same root as dismissal) urges us to get out there into the world. The ringing of the Angelus both inside and outside the church at the moment of consecration, signals the fact that what is happening is not divorced from the world's life, but is a special moment revealing the real presence of Christ to be discovered at all times and in all people. This has already been illustrated in Benedict's Rule and the hymn writer, Maurice Frank Campbell Willson, reinforces the theme in these lines:

Upon thy table, Lord, we place
These symbols of our work and thine,
Life's food won only by thy grace,
Who giv'st to all the bread and wine.

Within these simple things there lie
The height and depth of human life,
Our inward thought, our tears and toil,
Our hopes and fears, our joy and strife.

In them we see the seamen's skill
That brought the storm-lashed ship to land,
The cargo slings, the railway lines,
All work of human head and hand.

Accept them, Lord; from thee they come;
We take them humbly at thy hand:
These gifts of thine for higher use
We offer, as thou dost command.

All life is thine: O give us faith
To know thee in the broken bread,
And drink with thee the wine of life,
Thou Lord supreme of quick and dead.

To thee we come; refresh thou us
With food from thy most holy board,
Until the kingdoms of this world
Become the kingdom of the Lord.

- Hymns and Psalms 628
(including, as verse 3, lines from the original version)

THE LORD'S SUPPER and **HOLY COMMUNION** emphasise the fellowship aspect of the Sacrament, and when we read about the life of the early Christian Church in The Acts of the Apostles it is apparent that the breaking and sharing was part of an experiment in communal living.

> All whose faith had drawn them together held everything in common: they would sell their property and possessions and make a general distribution as the need of each required. With one mind they kept up their daily attendance at the temple, and, breaking bread in private houses, shared their meals with unaffected joy.
>
> – Acts 2.44–46

It seems likely that what is known now by these different names was preceded in the early Christian Church by a meal intended to be shared in Christian Love. The **Agape** or **Love-Feast** was causing problems at Corinth and in his First Letter to the Corinthians, chapter 11, Saint Paul rebukes their excesses and lack of real sharing during their meals together. For many centuries the Agape disappeared from Christian Worship, but was preserved by Moravian Christians who separated from the Church of Rome in the late fourteenth century. Moravian Missionaries took the custom to America where in August 1737 John Wesley, who was visiting Georgia, was introduced to it in Savannah.

> After evening prayers, we joined with the Germans in one of their love-feasts. It was begun and ended with thanksgiving and prayer, and celebrated in so decent and solemn a manner as a Christian of the apostolic age would have allowed to be worthy of Christ.
>
> – JOHN WESLEY, *Journal*

This so impressed Wesley that, following his conversion experience in May 1738, he visited a Moravian Settlement in Germany and experienced the Love-Feast again. During his travels recorded in the *Journal*, Love-Feasts are frequently mentioned. There was no formal liturgy, but according to Frank Baker in his book *Methodism and the Love-Feast* a familiar pattern emerged:

Hymn
Prayer
Grace (sung)
Bread distributed by stewards
Collection for the poor
Circulation of loving-cup
Address by the presiding minister
Testimonies and verses of hymns
Spontaneous prayers and verses of hymns
Closing exhortation by the minister
Hymn
Benediction

The physical ingredients of the meal among the Moravians at first were bread and wine, though the wine was later replaced by tea in order to make the Agape quite distinct from the Eucharist. Similarly in Methodist usage the beverage has usually been water (and occasionally tea), shared from a two-handled mug passed round from hand to hand. The food has varied from bread or biscuit to semi-sweet buns. On one notable occasion at Whitby, in 1770, the bread ran short and William Ripley bought gingerbread to supply the deficiency. In London individual buns were provided. A widespread tradition soon arose, however, that a kind of 'seed-bread' was the thing. In most places this was specially baked

for the purpose, witness an entry in the Keighley Circuit accounts for 1779: 'Four new tins for love-feast cakes, 6s.' The food was served from trays or dishes, or even brought round in clothes baskets. For when a thousand or more people were each to be served with a slice of seed-bread ample provision must be made. In his *Autobiographical Recollections* Dr Benjamin Gregory describes how in the early Victorian era the stewards would visit the manse bringing 'several basketsful of dainty seed-bread', left-overs from the quarterly love-feast, for consumption by the minister's children; not in this case clothes-baskets, however, but the little basket-work trays used for the love-feast, examples of which may be seen in the Keighley Museum.

– FRANK BAKER, *Methodism and the Love-Feast*

By 1920 Loving Cups had become relics often hidden away in vestry cupboards, but in more recent years they have been re-discovered as Christians of many different denominations have found this fellowship meal to be a means of Grace and a form of inter-communion.

When we say, 'Give us this day our daily bread' or sing, 'Bread of heaven, feed me now and ever more', or receive bread and wine, we are making real connections between bodily and spiritual refreshment, for that bread and wine represent both.

Be gentle when you touch bread;
Let it not lie uncared for - unwanted.
So often bread is taken for granted,
There is so much beauty in bread -
    Beauty of sun and soil,
    Beauty of patient toil;
Winds and rain have caressed it,
    Christ often blessed it,
Be gentle when you touch bread.

Be loving when you drink wine;
So freely received and joyfully shared
In the spirit of him who cared.
Warm as a flowing river,
    Shining and clear as the sun;
    Deep as the soil of human toil.
The winds and the air caressed it;
    Christ often blessed it.
Be loving when you drink wine.

Old Scottish Verse

Therefore, we ought not to be surprised by the Church lengthening the cords of its tent to provide hospitality and refreshment. Far from being a diversion from gospel imperatives, it is in keeping with the title deeds of our faith and points us, in the words of a much-loved Post Communion Prayer, 'To the heavenly banquet prepared for all people.'

✻   ✻   ✻

I was delighted when a Methodist Minister and contemporary hymn writer, Andrew Pratt, responded quickly to my invitation to provide a hymn for this book which skilfully provides the necessary links.

It makes a banquet from a meal
When fellowship is shared with friends,
The tête-à-tête is blessed by God,
Our food and conversation blends.

The little café where we meet,
The welcome hubbub that we hear,
The sights and smells that bring delight
Are signs that God and love are near.

On special days we eat in style,
We celebrate with food and wine,
We meet with joy, give thanks and sing
To God of harvest, fruit and vine.

Yet every time we take a meal
The fact that we are being fed
Confirms that God has heard our prayer:
'Give us, each day, our daily bread'.

- ANDREW PRATT
© *Reprinted by permission of Stainer & Bell Ltd*

Suggested tunes: WILLIAMS and CORNISH

DIRECTORY

A–Z OF CHURCH CAFÉS DISCOVERED SO FAR

The majority of the questionnaires completed were meticulous in their detail and some were accompanied by covering letters, photographs and menus. I have endeavoured to be faithful to the substance of each return while having, of necessity, to minimise the content. This is particularly true regarding the range of food and drink available. I hope there is enough here to give you a taste or flavour of the atmosphere in church cafés, the smell of good food and the rest must be left to your imagination.

The words printed in italics usually come direct from the questionnaires submitted. Sometimes at the end of an entry there is a cross reference (e.g. See **What's in a Name?**) This could mean you will find more specific details about a café in this section, or simply more general information about the name. I hope this will provide additional interest for the reader especially where the cafés are set in a wider context.

How many church cafés there are throughout the UK remains unknown. At the end of the book there are some blank pages for readers to list cafés already known to them or discovered in the future which do not appear in this directory. Please enable me to share this information in an occasional update pamphlet. For this I will need the basic details only and if possible the name of a local contact person.

The retired vicar who told me he would go the length of the country for bread pudding must seek until he finds!

ALTRINCHAM

Altrincham Methodist Church
Barrington Road
Altrincham
Cheshire WA14 1HF

ICHTHUS COFFEE BAR

Open: Monday to Friday 10 a.m. - 2 p.m., Saturday 10 a.m. - 2 p.m.
Staff: 1 full time and 9 volunteers (more on Saturdays)
Menu: Soup with roll and butter, hot pies, various. Pizzas, jacket potato
with butter fillings, chips, baked beans, sandwiches and toasted
sandwiches with a variety of fillings. Bacon baps (Saturdays only),
scone and butter, toasted teacake, toast, cakes, pies, ice cream.
Tea, coffee (decaffeinated available), fruit tea, chocolate, cold
drinks.

Started in 1993 and is used by 150 people a week who find
it mostly quiet and always friendly.

It is a comfortable meeting place and has enabled the church to
cater for outside organisations booking rooms, e.g. local busi-
nesses and borough council.

The coffee area is at the front of this well appointed modern building in
Altrincham town centre and clearly visible from the spacious car park. On
the back of each menu the word ICHTHUS is explained:

The Greek word for fish - each letter of the word in Greek is the
initial letter of a phrase which lies at the heart of our faith 'Jesus
Christ, God's Son, Saviour'. Nearly twenty centuries ago when
Christians were persecuted, the fish became a secret sign to identify
places where they would be sure of safety and welcome. We hope
that you will feel that welcome too as you visit the Ichthus Coffee
Bar - just one of the ministries of Altrincham Methodist Church.

ANDOVER

The Valley Church
31 Bridge Street
Andover
Hants SP10 1BE

THE BRIDGE COFFEE SHOP

Open: Monday to Saturday 10 a.m. - 4 p.m.
Staff: 2 full time, 7 part time,
and 7 volunteers

Menu: Bridge toasties (variety of fillings and served with side salad), toast, beans and cheese on toast, toasted teacakes, Bridge baked potatoes (fillings and side salad), Bridge salads, Bridge Bulge Builders! (biscuits, cakes, Danish pastries, gateaux/cheesecake). The sandwich menu or French stick torpedo offers a choice of seventeen different fillings and, apart from the usual, you will find Cumberland sausage and stuffing (hot or cold). World famous dubre!! Plus specials from the board and side salad at no extra charge. Vegetarian dishes clearly marked (V). Drinks include coffee, cappuccino, café latte or café mocha, coffee cafetiere, hot chocolate, cold drinks. The Bridge offers a special menu for children.

Started in 1999

... to offer an alternative way of reaching the public in Andover with the gospel ... Good food, good drinks, relaxed atmosphere, friendly welcoming staff.

See **Churches Working Together** and **Behind the Scenes**

ASHBOURNE

THE CORNERSTONE

Ashbourne Methodist Church
36 Church Street
Ashbourne
Derbyshire

Open: Thursday 10 a.m. – 3 p.m., Friday 10 a.m. – 3 p.m.,
Saturday 10 a.m. – 4 p.m.
Staff: 40 volunteers
Menu: Soup/bread, sandwiches, home-made cakes, teacakes, biscuits, tea, coffee, hot chocolate, fizzy drinks, juice.

Started in 1998.

The coffee shop had been a vision for a number of years as an Outreach Centre ... During a large renovation programme, the vision became a reality ... We have renovated a derelict property and provided a haven of welcome ... Friendly, relaxed atmosphere, very clean, not expensive ... In the first two years we served approximately 20,000 customers ... Has brought people together in a common purpose ... Made the church more visible in the town ... Brought new people to the church ... People on the edge of the congregation are being encouraged to take an active role in the church ... Learning to care for each other ... Pamphlets, books, cards available ... We advertise Bible Study Courses etc.

See **What's in a Name?**

ASHFORD

CENTREPIECE CHURCH (Methodist/United Reformed)

Bank Street
Ashford
Kent

Open: Saturday 10 a.m. - 12 noon
Staff: 24 volunteers
Menu: Coffee, tea, squash, cakes, cheese scones, cheese rolls, biscuits.

Started in the 1950s to raise money. There is a weekly bric-a-brac stall. Those on low incomes appreciate this.

Friendly atmosphere. People to talk to. Reasonable prices. Between 40 and 150 people enjoy what is provided ... It is never quiet ... The friendships among volunteers are very strong ... Integrates people into the church fellowship ... An opportunity to share faith.

BAILDON

WESLEY'S

Baildon Methodist Church
Newton Way
Baildon

Open: Monday to Friday 10 a.m. - 4 p.m., Saturday 9.30 a.m. - 12 noon
Staff: 2 part time and 80 volunteers
Menu: Monday to Friday lunches are served with a choice of main course and pudding. Snacks and sandwiches are served all day.

Started in its present form in 1995.

We had been open before as a church/community centre serving coffee and lunch once a week for pensioners. Decided to expand on this ... Warm, friendly, good food, can stay as long as you want, meet friends ... 50-70 a day come and others using the building for activities ... Quite a significant number of customers have volunteered to help and through that (and other routes) have come to church ... It's a meeting point for lots of people and unique in the community ... People are more aware of what the church is about and doing.

During a development scheme a few bits of the old church building were chopped off and vestries were redesigned. The space between church and hall was then used to provide a large reception/foyer/coffee lounge with book kiosk and modern kitchen to link the two buildings and provide high-standard accommodation for all-day community support work and counselling.

See **What's in a Name?**

BAKEWELL

MONDAY MORNING COFFEE

Bakewell Methodist Church
Matlock Road
Bakewell
Derbyshire

Open: Every Monday 10 a.m. – 12 noon (market day)
Bank Holiday Mondays 10 a.m. – 2 p.m.
Staff: 40 volunteers
Menu: Coffee, tea, biscuits, scones, squash (more choice on Bank Holidays).

Started in 1987 when the church was embarking on a redevelopment pro-gramme and the minister saw a busy Bakewell on Market Day and a closed church. The Revd Albert Harbey was the prime instigator. The busyness on the outside is now reflected on the inside with 200–300 people passing through on a typical Monday.

Friendly with welcoming waitresses ... Good place to meet friends ... A recognised port of call in Bakewell – made the church well known ... People are made aware through notices and posters of the work going on in the church and other associations.

A charity stall is a regular feature each week, organised by a different charity who are given the facility. Every tenth week they are also given the money from the coffee morning.

BASINGSTOKE

London Street United Reformed Church
20 London Street
Basingstoke
Hants   RG21 7NU
www.wiljamfsnet.co.uk/loust-hp.htm

THE OASIS

Open: Wednesday 10 a.m. - 2 p.m., Thursday 10 a.m. - 2 p.m.
Staff: 12 volunteers
Menu: Coffee, tea, cans of soft drinks, milk etc., cakes, biscuits, crisps.
All-day breakfast, baked potatoes with fillings, ploughman's, fresh
cut sandwiches, salads.

Started in 1996 to provide a peaceful Oasis for anyone seeking light refreshments.

*We do not hurry customers ... Stay until closing time if you wish ...
friendly service, good food, a listening ear, nice clean premises,
church open for prayer, faith building ... The teams working together
build relationships ... Regular customers become friends ... All kinds
of people come in from the homeless to business people, from
families to the isolated.*

Christian cards and books for sale.

BATH

Manvers Street Baptist Church
Bath
BA1 1JW

OPEN HOUSE COFFEE SHOP

Open: Monday to Saturday 10 a.m. - 4 p.m.
Staff: 4 full time and 60 volunteers serving 150 people per day
Menu: (12 - 2 p.m.) meat dish of the day, vegetarian dish of the day plus
soup and jacket potatoes with various fillings, dessert (throughout
the day), sandwiches, toasted sandwiches, bacon sandwiches,
toast, cakes and biscuits. Tea, coffee, (regular, expresso, cappuccino), hot chocolate, Horlicks, Ovaltine, mineral water, milk,
canned drinks etc.

Started in 1992 to serve as a ministry of hospitality.
*A warm, friendly place, a safe place to be listened to ...
Reasonable prices for good quality food ... An openness to
the community ... It has brought a lot of challenges that*

don't always equate with being a benefit ... It has raised questions and caused us to re-evaluate our purpose as a church ... People from all walks of life find it a benefit and also appreciate the open door from the coffee shop into the church for quiet prayer and reflection.

See **Vital Links** and **Behind the Scenes**

BEDFORD

Bunyan Meeting Free Church
Mill Street
Bedford
MK40 3EU

OPEN DOORS

Open: Tuesday to Saturday 10 a.m. - 4 p.m.
Staff: 24 volunteers
Menu: Tea, coffee, soft drinks, light refreshments.
Lunches served on Wednesdays.

Started in 1988 to provide refreshments for visitors who came to the church and museum to commemorate the tercentenary of John Bunyan's death.
It provides a warm welcome and a peaceful haven close to the town centre and refreshments at very reasonable prices ... The staffing arrangements have brought together church members and friends who otherwise would have had little contact with the church during the week ... We feel that this is a valuable community service project - we have many regular customers ... Several people have started to worship with us as a result of their contact with Open Doors and there has been a change of attitude towards the church.
Open Doors makes an annual contribution to Bedford Care for the Homeless and Rootless.

See **What's in a Name?**

BEDWAS

Bethel Baptist Church
1 Church Street
Bedwas, Caerphilly
CF83 8EA

THE ROCK

Open: Monday to Saturday 10 a.m. - 4.30 p.m. (except Wednesday)
Staff: One full time, 45 volunteers

Menu: Sandwiches (egg and mayonnaise, tuna, ham, cheese and pickle, salmon, bacon, cheese and tomato on brown or white bread, butter or low-fat spread). Hot Savouries served with or without salad garnish, toasted sandwiches, soup of the day, toast with beans, cheese or egg. A variety of sweets with warnings of traces of nuts and if dietary requirements needed then assistance may be given. Drinks: variety of coffees and teas e.g. cappuccino (cream or milk), Earl Grey, Darjeeling; milk shakes, juice, squash, pop, hot chocolate, all available to take away.

Started in 2001 after a God-given vision to the local Baptist Fellowship to reach out to the local community expressing God's love.

Closer links with community has raised the involvement level ... Church seen as being more relevant ... Expanded view of wider church, more links with other Christians.

There is a good book/gift shop with excellent service. The good food reasonably priced and the ambience of the centre has made an instant impact. A café regular writes:

Rock Café in Bedwas has celebrated its first anniversary and is such a success. It has brought Christians together for a start. Now business people have found it and they too join in the friendly banter. We really do have fun.

BELFAST

Belfast Central Mission
Grosvenor House
5 Glengall Street

THE SCALLOP SHELL

Belfast BT12 5AD

Open: Monday to Friday 8 a.m. – 3 p.m.
Staff: 7 full time and 2 volunteers
Menu: Morning coffee, full Ulster fry, scones, traybakes, lunches, filled rolls, sandwiches etc., soft drinks, coffee, tea and hot chocolate.

Started in 1996 to create an interface between the church and the general public by providing a street-front café in a newly decorated building. Also to provide catering for the conference and training centre.

Made the church more aware of those on the outside and to non-church people, the church is seen as more user friendly ... Provides a service to office workers and shoppers ... Lovely atmosphere, nice friendly staff and good food.

See **Vital Links**

BERKHAMSTED
(Churches Together)
Post Office, Bookshop, Coffee Shop

268 High Street
Berkhamsted
Herts
HP4 1AG

THE WAY INN CHRISTIAN CENTRE

Open: Monday to Saturday 9 a.m. – 5.30 p.m.
Staff: 11 full time. A large number of volunteers of whom at least 2 are on duty at any one time.
Menu: Tea, coffee and cakes at all times. Tea includes decaffeinated, Assam, Darjeeling or Earl Grey, herbal or fruit tea. Coffee includes instant, decaffeinated, cappuccino, expresso, fresh ground filter. Hot chocolate, cold drinks. Hot lunches – usually a choice of two meat dishes and one vegetarian, jacket potatoes with choice of fillings, toasted sandwiches, omelettes, salads, children's menu – frankfurters, waffles, baked beans etc. Choice of three sweets or ice cream.

Started in 1990 as an ecumenical venture supported by Baptists, Methodists, Anglican, United Reformed, Roman Catholic, Society of Friends and Salvation Army Churches.

Friendly atmosphere, good value for money, some elderly customers come every day for a hot meal ... Opportunity for conversation and sharing of problems.

The Way Inn also includes a bookshop and post office.

See **Churches Working Together**

WAY
INN

27

BILSTON

Bilston Methodist Church
Bow Street
Bilston
West Midlands, WV14 5LZ

OASIS

Open: Monday and Friday 10 a.m. - 2 p.m.
Staff: 12 volunteers
Menu: Tea, coffee, chocolate, cup-a-soups, squash, biscuits, crisps, confectionary, no cooked food.

Started in 1994.

There was a need to widen our horizons into all ages in the community ... A mums and toddlers group was proving difficult to continue and it seemed a good idea to provide a room where all ages could be accommodated ... It's friendly, gives opportunity to meet others, especially folks who live on their own, tea and coffee very cheap ... Strengthened understanding between people in the Sunday congregation and those who do not attend worship.

As a result of requests at Oasis a short period of worship has been introduced on Fridays and a Bible Study on Wednesdays. The community has become more aware of the church presence and it's given them a focus in the Methodist Church. New and nearly new clothes and bric-a-brac are sold.

It's an Oasis where you can pop in for a drink and a chat and possibly get a bargain and sense the presence of Jesus.

BIRMINGHAM

United Reformed Church Centre
Carrs Lane
Birmingham

DALE PANTRY CAFETERIA

Open: Monday to Friday 9.30 a.m. - 2.30 p.m.
(except Bank Holidays and around Christmas)
Staff: 2 full time, 5 part time and 10 volunteers
Menu: Breakfasts, snacks, cooked lunches, sandwiches and baguettes, tea, coffee and cold drinks.

Started in 1972 when the present building was opened, but its origins go back to a soup kitchen opened in the previous building in the 1930s.

To meet a need for affordable food in the city centre ... To encourage contact between the church and the city ... The Church Centre is busy every day with people passing through ... Plenty of challenging visual material on display, especially Christian Aid material ... About 500 people a week enjoy good food at reasonable prices in a friendly atmosphere ... A lot of regulars and people meeting friends. Also people needing support or counselling ... One regular at Sunday lunchtime was heard to say, 'I'm fussy who cooks my food, so that's why I come here.'

See **What's in a Name?**

BLACKPOOL

New Central Methodist Church
Adelaide Street West
Blackpool
Lancs FY1 4SR

COFFEE SHOP

Open: Tuesday to Saturday 10 a.m. – 4.30 p.m.
Staff: 57 volunteers serving 100 people per day in the winter
and 200 people per day in the summer
Menu: Tea, coffee, chocolate, minerals, milk, soup, crisps, biscuits, cake, savouries.

Started in 1974 for outreach purposes.
People come to share in the peace we offer in a busy town centre and the fellowship they find with us.
The Coffee Shop has been the means of developing Fellowship Groups including staff and customers. A midday service is held in the Coffee Shop on Wednesdays. Some marriage blessings have been held at this service and baptisms have also come as a direct result of it. Volunteers are drawn from different churches in the town. An open-door policy operates within the Coffee Shop for homeless and needy people. A Town Centre Chaplaincy operates as part of the Coffee Shop ministry.
There is a sense of Jesus at work in the Town Centre and we are able to give our time in service to others ... The opportunity to share our stories with new Christians and to show to all that the church has a mission in serving the community.

BLACKPOOL

First Step Community Centre
Methodist Church Buildings
Dickson Road
Blackpool
NIBBLES AT CLAREMONT

FY1 2AP

Open: Monday to Friday 10 a.m. - 4 p.m.

Staff: 4 full time (including 2 supervisors seconded from Blackpool Social Services) and 4 volunteers per day with a learning disability

Menu: Home-made soup with bread, sandwiches (ham and salad, turkey and salad, Lancashire cheese and fruit chutney, egg mayonnaise, tuna mayonnaise, carrot and humus, cottage cheese and salad). Jacket potatoes (various fillings and side salad), daily specials, home-made cakes. Tea, herbal teas (variety of flavours), coffee (regular or decaffeinated), hot chocolate, mineral water, fruit juice, cordial.

Started early in 2001, the café is in partnership with Nibbles Café in Mereside and provides vocational training for adults with learning difficulties.
   It's different!

See **Vital Links**

BOLTON

The Victoria Hall
Methodist Mission
Knowsley Street
Bolton
THE RIDGWAYS COFFEE SHOP AND GIFT SHOP

BL1 2AS

Open: Tuesday 10 a.m. - 4 p.m., Wednesday 10 a.m. - 1.30 p.m. Thursday 10 a.m. - 4 p.m.

Staff: 10 volunteers

Menu: Tea, coffee, hot chocolate, juice, sandwiches, scones, cakes and biscuits.

Started in 1999 as a means of opening up the front entrance of the building on a busy main street in the town centre.
   Quiet friendly atmosphere ... Handy for local bus stop ... We have a small prayer chapel at the front of the building. This is frequently

used by customers, many of whom attend the mid-week service held there ... The Gift Shop sells mainly Christian based items ... Church-related literature available on all tables.

The Mission Café (Ridgway Gates Entrance)

Open: Tuesday, Thursday, Saturday 10 a.m. – 2 p.m.

Staff: 3 full time, 8 church volunteers and 20 BAND volunteers-in-training (NB not Brass Band! – Bolton Association Network of Drop-Ins offering training in catering, health and hygiene to those who experience mental health problems and providing the café with volunteer staff)

Menu: Sandwiches and barmcakes (cold and hot) with various fillings and salad garnish, soup, toasted sandwiches, jacket potatoes, vegetarian. Dish of the day. Toast, toasted teacakes, egg or beans on toast, pudding of the day, cakes. Tea, coffee, hot chocolate served with whipped cream and marshmallows, pop, cordial. Daily specials board of selected hot meals, pudding of the day, a children's menu is available.

Started in 1999.

The organisation BAND was looking for kitchen premises in which to carry out its training. We were looking for more people to staff our busy café ... Hot, cheap meals. Friendly service. Always someone ready to chat with if required.

Over 100 come daily. BAND has branched out and now does buffets for anyone booking rooms at the Victoria Hall. The church library is situated in the café. The Victoria Hall is an integral part of the new Victoria Gardens Development Plan.

BOURNEMOUTH

PLACE NEXT DOOR

Salvation Army
1 Latimer Road
Winton, Bournemouth
Dorset BH9 1JY

Open: Monday to Friday 10 a.m – 2.30 p.m.

Staff: 2 full time, 4 part time and 3 volunteers serving 250 people a day

Menu: Choice of 3 or 4 main meals (served between 12.15 and 2 p.m.), snacks (jacket potatoes, salads, sandwiches, toasted sandwiches) and breakfasts served all day.

Started in 1988 to serve the community practically as well as spiritually.

It is a welcoming and friendly atmosphere where people can make friends, receive help if needed or just meet a friend for a coffee or meal ... Salvation Army members are offering their service to God and meeting people in the Centre who would not normally go to church. Some have been introduced to the church through the Centre ... The community has benefited from reasonably priced meals, particularly elderly people living alone ... We also provide free meals for the homeless once a week (approximately 80 people) ... Catering for events on a large scale ... Summer coach parties, dinners etc.

The Place Next Door was originally an ice cream factory. It was purchased by the Salvation Army in 1987 and following refurbishment now provides a centre for community needs just off the main Winton Shopping Centre in a largely residential area of 30,000 people. People of all ages converge on the centre from all walks of life and with many different needs.

BROADSTAIRS

Queens Road Baptist Church
Broadstairs
GAP COMMUNITY PROJECT   Kent
CAFÉ GAP   CT10 1NU

Open: Monday 10 a.m. – 12.15 p.m., Friday 10.30 a.m. – 1.30 p.m.
Menu: Soup, create a meal from a variety of choices (burger in a bun, chips, *burger beef, *burger minted lamb, bacon, *sausage, ham, soft roll, egg, beans, peas (*freshly made by a local butcher). Jacket potatoes with a variety of fillings. Bottomless cups of tea or coffee.

Café Gap

Friendly, central, good food at low prices, place to meet friends. Has become an integral part of the community attracting a cross-section of people e.g. workers, school excluders, homeless, elderly, shoppers. A Christian presence and influence at the centre of town and outside the main bus stop. Part of 'Bridging the Gap'. A Thanet Community Project – an effort to connect with people at their point of need. The Gap Project includes :-

    Sit and be fit ...

        4-2-6 ... (for young people)

            D-Jing Workshop ...

                Rainbow Crèche ...

                    Break Dancing Workshop ...

                        IT Works ...

                          Youth Club

Project 10 and Project 15 (school excluders programme). Basic Skills Project (one-to-one literacy tuition for adults). The project recently won top prize in a competition organised by the Kent Messenger newspaper group and Barclays Bank. More than 50 volunteers are involved in Gap, which helps all age groups from babes-in-arms to over eighties. Those on the mailing list receive a prayer letter several times a year.

See **Behind the Scenes**

BROMLEY

The Salvation Army, Bromley
Temple Corps
Ethelbert Road
Bromley

SALLY'S PLACE

Kent BR1 1HU

Open: Monday to Friday 10 a.m. – 3.45 p.m.
      Saturday 10 a.m. – 12.15 p.m.
Staff: 2 full time and 30 volunteers
Menu: Hot and cold drinks, sandwiches, toasties, cakes, biscuits etc.

Started in 1995 to be a bridge to the community and a means of fund-raising.

Provides a good opportunity for members of our corps to work together and share in service ... Friendly, welcoming atmosphere ... Reasonable prices ... A number of people have linked with worship opportunities as a result of the café/shop ... Many people have benefited from the contacts and friendships made in the café/shop.

BROMSGROVE

Bromsgrove Methodist Centre
19 Stratford Road
Bromsgrove
COFFEE SHOP
Worcester B60 1AS

Open: Each weekday 10 a.m. - 3.30 p.m., Saturday 10 a.m. - 12.30 p.m.
Staff: Volunteers, serving an average of 50 people per day.
Menu: Freshly cut ham and cheese rolls, sandwiches, various soups,
beans on toast, tea, coffee, chocolate, fruit teas, soft drinks, a
selection of confectionary.

 Quiet friendly atmosphere, children are most welcome.
Started in 1984 when three churches came together to
form the Methodist Centre in Bromsgrove. A site close
to the town centre provided the opportunity to build for
the whole community, not just for a Sunday congregation
and church-based groups. A large glass screen with a
central cross, through which the town can be seen,
demonstrates the dedication of the building to the whole
community. In a building where nothing is fixed and
everything is made to move easily, it's not surprising that the foyer is also
the coffee shop.

Great sense of fellowship ... We have patrons who would perhaps not
enjoy a hot meal at home, but will share a meal here ... We have a
hard core of regular patrons who find fellowship and friendship here
... We try to give local information where needed and there is a lend-
ing library in the café.

BURNLEY

Central Methodist Church
Hargreaves Street
Burnley
COFFEE BAR
Lancashire

Open: Monday to Saturday 10 a.m. - 4 p.m.
except Tuesday 10 a.m. - 1 p.m.
Staff: 50 volunteers
Menu: Coffee, tea, Bovril, hot chocolate plus small bottles of pop and
still fruit drinks. Toasted bread, teacakes and currant bread. A
wide range of biscuits.

Started when the church was opened in 1967 because the Joseph Rank Benevolent Fund offered to give £1 for every £1 raised by the church providing a coffee bar for public use was incorporated in the new building. Between 100 and 120 people per day come to the Coffee Bar.

People like the friendly and caring atmosphere ... The prices are reasonably cheap and it is very popular with the elderly ... It is noted for being the best cup of coffee in town ... We now have several of our customers who help regularly on the Coffee Bar rota ... Lonely people have made friends here and now meet on a regular basis ... We are always willing to accommodate local charities e.g. Poppy Appeal, hospice etc.

BUXTON

Buxton Methodist Church
Market Place
Buxton
CHURCH IN THE MARKET PLACE CAFÉ
Derbyshire SK17

Open: (Market Days) Tuesday 10 a.m. – 12.30 p.m.
Saturday 10 a.m. – 12.30 p.m.
Staff: 20 volunteers (Tuesday), 49 volunteers (Saturdays)
Menu: Tea, coffee, chocolate, juices and squash, cup-a-soups served with bread, toast, toasted teacakes, biscuits and cakes.

The Saturday Café was opened in 1971 following the amalgamation of two churches on the Market Place site (formerly known as Wesley).

Funds were needed to refurbish the church and many events were organised including a coffee morning with men serving the coffee wearing black and white and using silver coffee pots ... After this it was decided to open on a regular basis and volunteers were called for.

Saturday is Buxton's traditional Market Day, but in the early 1980s a Tuesday Market was started and a café opened to serve shoppers. Since 1989 there has been an informal service on Tuesday Mornings and following the Vision 2000 Development Scheme, numerous community groups meet on the premises – so both Saturday and Tuesday Cafés are busy (approximately 300 people over two mornings). The church is ideally situated and the café attracts both locals and tourists.

*Relaxing ... cheap prices ... Meeting place for friends and families ...
clean pleasing surroundings ... No pressure to vacate tables ... Some
customers will sit and talk for one-and-a-half hours ... Main benefit
is church folk and other helpers meet together and get to know and
care for each other. Relationships are more easily established over a
shared task, however menial.*

BUXTON

Faith in Fairfield Project
135 Victoria Park Road
Fairfield, Buxton
SK17 7PE

THE PEPPERPOT CAFÉ

Open: Monday to Friday 9 a.m. to 2 p.m.
Staff: 17 volunteers
Menu: Tea, coffee, variety of soft drinks. Hot
snacks (toasties, bacon baps, jacket potatoes). Full breakfasts, meal of the day at
lunchtime. Take-away snacks.

Started in 2001 as part of the wider Faith in Fairfield
Project. Based in a shop on the Fairfield Estate, supported by Anglican and Methodist Churches.
*Bright, friendly, informal ... Many of the customers
are greeted by name ... Has enabled the churches to discover the
community and the community to discover the churches.*

See **Vital Links**

CAMBORNE

Wesley Methodist Church
Chapel Street
Camborne
TR14 8EG

CHURCH CENTRE CAFÉ

Open: Monday to Friday 9 a.m. – 3.30 p.m., Saturday 10 a.m. – 11.30 a.m.
Staff: 3 full time
Menu: (Monday to Friday mornings) English breakfast, soup and roll,
coffee, tea. (Midday) three course meals, salads, jacket potatoes,
fish and chips etc. (Saturday mornings) coffee only.

Started in 1993 in response to a vision of need seen by the Revd Edgar Daniel who was minister of the church. Now 150 people can be expected each week and 110 meals on wheels are taken out.

Food – high standard – fair price – great value ... Friendly service ... 100 per cent improvement in fellowship of the church as a result of the café ... Additional attendance at services.

Emmanuel United Reformed Church
Trumpington Street
Cambridge
CB2 1RR

FAIR SHARES CAFÉ

Open: Wednesday, Thursday, Friday 10.30 – 3 p.m.
(also when there are special projects, exhibitions at other times)
Staff: Full time and volunteers working together
Menu: (10.30 a.m. – 3 p.m.) coffee, tea, cold drinks, cakes. (Noon – 2 p.m.) lunch: menu soup of the day with French bread and butter (side salad), jacket potatoes with fillings – butter, cheese, cheese and ham, cottage cheese and mushroom, meat-free chilli, baked beans, bacon, vegetable curry, tuna and sweetcorn. White or brown bread rolls with fillings. Quiche Lorraine, vegetable quiche of the day (with new potatoes and salad). Snacks on toast.

Started in 2000 as part of a major initiative to develop ministry in the city centre.

Warm and welcoming. Good service in a very pleasant environment. Quality food – not expensive ... The fact that the café is run in partnership with MENCAP means a lot to people ... Growing contact with community – has put Emmanuel on the map and brought people into the church.

See **Vital Links**

CANTERBURY

St Andrews United Reformed Church
Watling Street
Canterbury

OASIS

Kent CT1 2UA

Open: Wednesday 10.30 a.m. – 2 p.m. (in new church since March 2001
and intending to open 6 days a week)
Staff: 24 volunteers
Menu: Tea, coffee, hot chocolate, cold drinks, toast, beans on toast,
jacket potatoes with fillings, ploughman's, sandwiches (variety
of fillings), desserts (ice cream, cakes), daily specials.

Started in 1995. Open to anyone who wants to stop for
peace and quiet and maybe some faith sharing.
*No pressure to eat/drink and go ... Convenient to the
car park and shopping centre ... Helped in the family feel
of the church ... Used for evening youth events.*

CARDIFF

Beulah United Reformed Church
Beulah Road
Rhiwbina

THE MARGARET WHITTAKER LOUNGE

Cardiff CF14

*Margaret Whittaker, a much respected member, willed her house to
Beulah Church. This coincided with the Centenary of our present
worship building. Margaret's generosity encouraged our congregation to raise additional funds with which to mark the milestone and
provide suitable premises for the next century. We have therefore
developed our inadequate rear vestries to create a modern lounge for
church and community, a church office, and given a face-lift to our
worship centre. We give thanks to God for Margaret's generosity.*

Open: Monday, Wednesday, Thursday, Friday, Saturday
10 a.m. – 1 p.m. (on Tuesday mornings house-
bound folk are brought in for a coffee morning)
Staff: 80 volunteers
Menu: Toasted sandwiches, soup, teacakes, crumpets, toast, Welsh cakes,
scones, crisps, biscuits, home-made cakes, tea, coffee, soft drinks.

38

Started in 1991 to provide a quiet place in the middle of the village where people can meet together and enjoy fellowship in the lounge. There is no obligation to buy food!

For people coming into the lounge it is sometimes the first step into the church. There is a short service in the church on Wednesday mornings.

Community links are strengthened through the Rhiwbina Good Neighbours Office on the premises. The lounge serves Traidcraft coffee and tea and also Traidcraft goods. There are special links with Romania.

CARDIFF   Rhiwbina Baptist Church
                                                L'n Ucha, Rhiwbina
THE OLIVE BRANCH   Cardiff

Open: Monday to Saturday 9.30 a.m. – 4.15 p.m.
Staff: 3 full time and 15 volunteers
Menu: Coffee, tea, juices, hot chocolate, toasties, jacket potatoes, soup, sandwiches, quiche, corned beef pie, home-made cakes, puddings, crumble, cheesecakes and gateaux.

Started in 1986 as a local meeting point in the village and now catering for 600 people a week.

It has given the church a purpose, vision, direction ... A haven for lonely people ... Worth its weight in gold.

Money raised to provide books for a local school and for supporting mission work.

CARDIFF   Excalibur Drive
                                                        Thornhill
                                                          Cardiff
THORNHILL CENTRE   CF4 9GA

Open: Monday to Friday 10 a.m. – 4 p.m., Saturday 10 a.m. – 1 p.m.
Staff: 8 part-time and 5 volunteers
Menu: Sandwiches (variety of fillings), freshly toasted sandwiches, soup, toasted teacakes, toasted crumpets, toasted bagels, gateaux and cakes, Thayers ice creams (award winners!), coffee (including

expresso, cappuccino, decaffeinated), tea (including Earl Grey), hot chocolate, cold drinks.

Started in 1998 when the centre was opened and now attracts 100 people a day. Just like the Coffee Lounge and Café, the atmosphere in the Centre as a whole can vary from a busy hurly burly to tranquil peace and quiet.

Helped build bridges with the community ... Feel at home and meet friends ... Relax and have fun ... Find meaning and new purpose in life.

CARLISLE

DOVES COFFEE LOUNGE AND FAIR TRADE SHOP

Churches Together in Carlisle
Church of Scotland, St Andrew's Centre
Chapel Street, Carlisle
Cumbria

Open: Monday to Friday 10 a.m. - 2 p.m.
Staff: 3 full time and 50-60 volunteers from all churches in Carlisle
Menu: Morning special: tea, coffee with scone or toast. Soup of the day, chef's special of the day and a vegetarian choice. Jacket potatoes, sandwiches, scrambled egg, bacon, rolls, freshly baked scones and home-made tray bakes.

Started in 1994 as a meeting point and to promote fairly traded produce.

See **Churches Working Together**

CARLISLE

OASIS COFFEE SHOP

St Paul's Elim Pentecostal Church
Lonsdale Street
Carlisle
Cumbria CA1 1BJ

Open: Tuesday to Friday 10 a.m. - 2 p.m.
Menu: Soup of the day with roll and butter, also soup to take away. Meal of the day (see board for details), pizza slice, corned beef pie, cheese pie (all with salad). Baked potatoes with a variety of

fillings. A selection of sixteen sandwich fillings and eleven toasted sandwiches (all available with salad), cakes and desserts (e.g. rock buns, fruit pie, tray bakes, lemon meringue, fruit flan, toasted teacake, Knickerbocker Glory, banana split, ice cream. Tea, coffee, hot chocolate, herbal tea, milk, milk shakes, lemonade, Coke, Lilt, Tango, Sprite.

Started in 1986 and now serving 75-100 people each day. *Cheap, friendly, nice atmosphere ... Made contacts for the church – some coming to salvation ... Provided employment for staff ... Age Concern, deaf, blind and disabled all use the café to 'bring' groups for coffee and meals ... Local businesses order sandwiches for lunchtime meetings ... Income has helped the church to sponsor a child through Tear Fund.*

CHARD

THE WELCOME BAP

Chard Baptist Church
Holyrood Street
Chard, Somerset
TA20 2AH

Open: Monday to Saturday 10 a.m. – 12 noon
Staff: 1 full time and 40 volunteers
Menu: Tea and Earl Grey tea, coffee, hot chocolate, cold drinks, milk shakes, cakes, scones, toasted teacakes, toast, crumpets, biscuits, ice cream.

Started to offer a shop window for the work of the church and to build bridges with the community.

It's a meeting place for a number of our own folk ... We have built up a good reputation in the town, got to know non-church customers and holiday makers ... They like the friendly atmosphere, cleanliness and helpful staff ... Our Prayer Request Box from customers of people they wish us to pray for is an encouragement.

CHELMSFORD

Trinity Methodist Church
Rainsford Road
Chelmsford, Essex
CM1 2XB

THE LINK

Open: Monday, Tuesday, Friday
Staff: 40 volunteers
Menu: Tea, coffee, fruit juice, Coke, squash, scones, biscuits. On Fridays
(12 - 1.30 p.m.) lunches are served offering soup and roll, dish of
the day, salads, sausages, hot dogs, jacket potatoes (various fillings) puddings etc.

Started in 1984 when The Link building at Trinity (formerly a greengrocer's
shop and then a builder's warehouse) was refurbished.
*User friendly atmosphere ... Has helped us to understand local needs
... Some people have joined the church as a result of coming
to The Link.*

All profits go to charity and to support the
church and its activities. Over eighteen
years £30,000 has been raised in spite of a
two course meal costing only £3.00!

CHELMSFORD

Central Baptist Church
Victoria Road South
Chelmsford
Essex

THE OASIS CAFÉ

Open: Tuesday to Saturday 10.30 a.m. - 1.30 p.m.
Staff: 29 volunteers
Menu: Tea, coffee, cappuccino, herbal tea, soup and rolls, sandwiches,
toasted sandwiches, pizza and salad, jacket potatoes with fillings,
toast, toasted teacake, scones, ice cream etc.

Started in 1991 in a town centre church as a ministry to passers by.
*Friendly staff, reasonable prices ... a working team each day get to
know each other better ... A number have joined Bible Study Courses
and started to come to services ... Provides a drop-in point for people
in need ... Now giving one day's profit each week to charity.*

42

Wesley Methodist Church
St John Street
Chester

OPEN DOOR

Open: Tuesday to Saturday 10 a.m. - 3 p.m.
Staff: 1 full time and 3 part time
Menu: (Tuesday and Wednesday) coffee, tea, biscuits, crisps, cakes.
(Thursday and Friday) also hot lunches and sandwiches.
(Saturday) a variety of food run by various fund-raising charity
groups.

Started in 1989 on a prime site between the shopping centre and the River
Dee in an attempt to be available to people throughout the week as
well as on Sundays. Between 750 and 1,000 people each week enjoy the
unhurried atmosphere which has given the church an additional sense of
purpose.

A project for prayer, caring, meeting ... Commitment through con-
tinued challenges ... Always a buzz - a centre for many groups to
benefit from ... Good display material around with a focus on
Christian themes.

Chesterfield Central Methodist Church
Saltergate
Chesterfield

CORNERSTONE BOOKSHOP AND COFFEE BAR

Open: Monday, Tuesday, Thursday, Friday, Saturday 10 a.m. - 4 p.m.
Staff: 60 volunteers
Menu: A reasonable range of hot and cold drinks (tea,
coffee, hot chocolate, soup, squash and canned
drinks). Light refreshments - all wrapped. Crisps,
plain and chocolate biscuits, muffins, chocolate,
rolls etc.

Started in 1985 when the church premises were extensively redeveloped as
a means of bringing people on to the premises. About 650 people a week
come to Cornerstone.

Our customers feel comfortable with the atmosphere we provide ...
Single people, often widows or widowers have found companionship
with each other and the staff ... There has never been any overt

attempt at evangelism, in trying to persuade or cajole people into church attendance, though some have come.

It has created a community spirit in the town centre and this is a benefit in itself.

See **What's in a Name?**

CHESTERFIELD

THE SAINTS

Parish Centre and Coffee Shop
All Saints Parish Church
3 St Mary's Gate, Chesterfield
Derbyshire S41 7TJ

Open: Monday to Saturday 10 a.m. - 4 p.m.
Staff: 24 volunteers serving 100 people per day
Menu: Sandwiches, cakes, scones, tea, coffee, orange, cans of pop.

Started in 1996 in the centre across the road from this historic church.
We are friendly and our cakes are all made in the kitchen upstairs.
... Visitors appreciate this lovely café so near to the church.

See **What's in a Name?**

CHESTER-LE-STREET

PARISH CENTRE

St Mary and St Cuthbert's Church
Chester-le-Street
County Durham
DH3 3YB

Open: Monday to Friday 10 a.m. - 2 p.m. (operated by church)
Saturday 10 a.m. - 2 p.m. (operated by church groups and charities for their own fund-raising)
Staff: 1 supervisor and volunteers serving 760 people per week
Menu: Cooked meals and salads, toasted sandwiches.

A good meeting place both for church members and non-church people ... Good value for money ... Friendships have developed ... The atmosphere is warm and welcoming ... A huge financial success, but this was not the idea when we opened ... Has gained members for the church.

CIRENCESTER

Cirencester Parish Church
3 Dollar Street
Cirencester
THE CORNERSTONE

Gloucestershire

Open: Monday to Saturday 9.30 a.m. - 5 p.m.
Staff: 1 full time and 36 volunteers
Menu: Tea, coffee, soft drinks, home-made cakes.

Started in 1991 as an extension of the ministry of Cirencester Parish Church. An opportunity to be of service to the local community and the many visitors to the town. The café is integral with the bookshop.

Friendly, welcoming atmosphere ... opportunity to sit and chat with friends including staff and volunteers ... Faith sharing through friendships developed.

See **What's in a Name?**

COVENTRY

Central Hall
Warwick Lane
Coventry
WESLEY'S COFFEE LOUNGE

CV1 2HA

Open: Monday to Saturday 10 a.m. - 3 p.m.
Staff: 3 full time and 40 volunteers
Menu: Range of snacks and meals e.g. jacket potatoes, cottage pie, lasagne, chef's special daily, hot and cold drinks.

Started in 1989 to begin the process of opening up the hall to the public and to provide hospitality in the city centre. Also catering for organisations using the hall. A meal voucher scheme operates for those in need.

Homely atmosphere - no background music - quality food ... has brought church volunteers together in a working fellowship ... Midweek worship attended by some people who come to the Coffee Lounge ... Has given us a renewed good reputation and financially underpinned much of our redevelopment work.

See **What's in a Name?**

CROSBY

CROSSROADS CENTRE

Churches Together in Crosby
Liverpool Road, Crosby
Liverpool L23

Open: Monday to Saturday 9.15 a.m. - 4.15 p.m.
Staff: 4 full time and 20 volunteers serving 350-500 a week
Menu: Snacks, cakes, ploughman's, pies, soup, sandwiches, baked
potatoes, toastie snacks, fruit pies, ice cream, tea, coffee.

Started in 1990 as a commercial venture involving six churches. It soon become a focal point within the community.
Volunteers from different churches work well together ... Many people come in each day share tables, a good cheap meal and are known by name ... problems shared ... a lot of laughter in the café.

See **Churches Working Together**

DAWLEY

Dawley Methodist Christian Centre
High Street
Dawley
Telford

COFFEE BAR

Open: Monday to Friday 9.30 a.m. - 1.30p.m.
Saturday 9.30 a.m. - 12.30 p.m.
Staff: 30 volunteers
Menu: Tea, coffee, cold drinks, crisps, biscuits, sandwiches made to
order. Toast, bacon and egg or what we think the customer
would like!

Started in 1987 in a new church building to open it up during the week.
Very popular on Friday market day (about 100).
Somewhere to meet friends, have a chat, a drink while waiting for a bus or taxi ... All friendly volunteers ... Gives the church financial help towards paying a caretaker and secretary. Helps us to send money to Mission Work and other organisations to raise money for charities ... Opportunities to share the faith with people.

Dorchester United Church
(Methodist / United Reformed)
Charles Street
Dorchester

NUMBER 51 COFFEE LOUNGE

Dorset

Open: Tuesday, Thursday, Friday 9.30 a.m. - 12.30 p.m., also on
Saturday when the church hall is not let for other charity events
(market day coffee morning in church hall on Wednesday)
Staff: 6 volunteers
Menu: Coffee, tea, hot chocolate, cold drinks, cakes, toast, teacakes.

Started in 2000 following a Church Visions Day. Amongst many other ideas
there emerged the need for a café. Being well placed opposite a public car
park the café is visible and used by visitors to the town.

*Friendly staff, excellent value for money ... New friendships have
been made among customers and volunteers ... Friends from other
churches have become involved ... Some volunteers have joined the
church.*

In September 1997 the church held a Visions Day when over 100 people
reflected together on the question, 'What does God want us to be and do
in the new millennium?' Amongst many other ideas there emerged the
need for a café. Three months later the shop next door was for sale and
the church decided to purchase No 51 Charles Street with the help of a
legacy from a church member. Over £60,000 was raised in two years
towards refurbishment and No 51 was opened in June 2000. It includes a
Christian Resources Centre and Exhibition Area. Redevelopment was not
restricted to No 51 - a new Quiet Room has been created near the rear
door into the church.

EASTLEIGH

Eastleigh Baptist Church
Wells Place Centre
Eastleigh, SO50 5LJ

WELLS PLACE COFFEE SHOP

Open: Tuesday to Friday 10 a.m. - 2 p.m. (term time)
Staff: Some full time or part time and 16 volunteers
Menu: Hot drinks, cakes, snacks, light lunches (soup, baguettes, jacket
potatoes etc.).

Started in 1998 as an outreach activity from a new church in the town centre.

High public profile - increased community contact - evangelistic and pastoral care opportunities ... Quiet atmosphere - restful - quality food - good toilet facilities ... Known meeting place in the town - disabled friendly ... Teamwork among the staff and a sense of servanthood.

EXETER

Palace Gate Centre
3 Palace Gate
Exeter
EX1 1JA

COFFEE SHOP

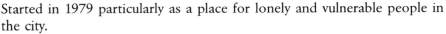

Open: Tuesday to Thursdays 10 a.m. - 2 p.m.
   (closed August)
Staff: 2 full time and 16 volunteers
Menu: Drinks and snacks available the whole time.
   Between 11.45 a.m. and 2 p.m. salads and a choice
   of four hot dishes.

Started in 1979 particularly as a place for lonely and vulnerable people in the city.

Cheap food, well cooked, warm friendly atmosphere ... Broken down barriers, haven for the vulnerable, focus of service for volunteers, some have come through to church membership ... Part of mission of the church to the city.

See **Churches Working Together**

GARSTANG

Garstang Methodist Church
Parkhill Road
Garstang,
Preston
PR3 1EL

THE MUSTARD SEED

Open: Tuesday 10 a.m. - 12 noon, Thursday 10 a.m. - 2 p.m.
   Saturday 10 a.m. - 12 noon
Staff: 25 volunteers

Menu: Fairtrade coffee, tea, assorted packet biscuits, orange squash, cakes, Lilt.

Started in 1991 and now recognised as a Fairtrade outlet. Profit distributed to Third World contacts.
Meeting point; friendly atmosphere; contributed to church growth and fellowship.

See **Vital Links**

GLASGOW   **Croftfoot Parish Pastoral Committee**
318 Croftpark Avenue
Croftfoot
Glasgow
COFFEE SHOP   **G44**

Open: Wednesday 10.30 a.m. - 12 noon
Staff: 18 volunteers
Menu: Cheese and biscuits, cakes, fruit loaves, tea, coffee and fruit juice.

Started in 1998 to encourage fellowship within the church and community. *Not in a passing trade situation. About 14-20 regulars who enjoy good home baking and a general chit chat. We hear of anyone needing help a lot earlier through the Coffee Shop ... We have been able to be generous to various projects.*

GLASGOW   **Freeland Drive**
Priesthill
Glasgow
JACOB'S WELL AND THRIFT SHOP   **G53**

Open: Wednesday 10 a.m. - 1 p.m.
        (March, April, May, Sept, Oct, Nov)
Staff: 6 volunteers
Menu: Soup and roll, home baking, tea, coffee, biscuits (free).

Started in 1996 to try and encourage the local community to come in for a friendly chat and to meet some of our church members hoping to give an insight into what our church stands for.

It has helped us become more aware of the community and its needs – meeting people on a one-to-one basis personalises the problems they face ... company for the elderly, faith sharing ... many a bargain found in the thrift shop.

GLOSSOP

The Geoffrey Allen Centre
The Jericho Project
Winster Mews
Gamesley, Glossop

COMMUNITY CAFÉ

Derbyshire SK13 0LU

Open: Monday to Friday 9 a.m. – 2 p.m., Saturday 9 a.m. – 12 noon
Staff: 3 part time, 10 volunteers, placement trainees from different providers serving 150–200 per week
Menu: Tea, coffee, cappuccino, milk shakes, cool drinks, jacket potatoes (various fillings), sandwiches, pies (cold and hot), salad, all-day breakfast, omelettes, main meals with daily special, cakes and desserts. Healthy options available and buffet and catering service.

Started in 1998 to a fill a gap in local social provision. A way of offering healthy food options in a locality with high poor health indications.
Good location, friendly atmosphere, variety of food ... contact point for conversation between church and community users ... information centre ... Provision of employment support and enabling people to find work ... cook-and-eat courses available.
Insight into 'normality' of church people through volunteers and non-church staff working together and equally the 'normality of local people on a council estate'. The café is the 'flagship' of the Jericho Project, an initiative of the Churches of St John's, Charlesworth; Holy Trinity, Dinting and Gamesley. The project seeks to work in partnership with the Gamesley community and with other agencies including health, education, youth and social services, generating new projects to enhance the lives of local people.

See **Behind the Scenes**

GREAT YARMOUTH   Christchurch Methodist / URC Church
                                                        King Street
                                                   Great Yarmouth
COFFEE SHOP   NR30 2HL

Open: Monday to Friday 10 a.m. - 2 p.m.
Saturday 10 a.m. -12 noon (coffee and cakes only)
Staff: 32 volunteers (some from the church and some from MENCAP
and MIND)
Menu: Sandwiches, soup, salads, coffee, tea, soft drinks, hot chocolate,
cakes, scones, jacket potatoes.

Started in 1990 as a way of reaching out into the community.
*Warm, friendly, peaceful, affordable ... Helps with upkeep of build-
ing and brings new people into the church ... Those who help make
time to sit and talk to customers ... NCH Action for Children and
Traidcraft use it as a base.*

GRIMSBY   Laceby Road Methodist Church
                                                          Grimsby

THE SIDE DOOR CAFÉ (Youth Outreach)

Open: Monday to Saturday
Staff: 1 full time youth worker and 8 volunteers
Menu: Soft drinks, toasted sandwiches, chips, toast, teacakes, cakes,
hot dogs, tea and coffee.

Started in 2000 as a Circuit youth outreach. The church is positioned on
the edge of a council estate.
*It's colourful ... We give time to the young people ... They feel wel-
come ... It's raised the profile of the church as a community building
... The church is suddenly the place to be seen in ... On Saturdays we
engage in challenging youth outreach with children who can be
difficult.*
The café is also used as a Circuit meeting place for youth activities, cell
groups, youth worship etc. Has put the church in touch with over sixty
young people a week.

High Street Methodist Church
Harpenden
Herts

WESLEY'S

Open: Monday to Thursday 10 a.m. – 12 noon,
Friday 10 a.m. – 4.30 p.m.
Saturday 10 a.m. – 12.30 p.m. (for charities)
Staff: 80 volunteers serving 30–40 per day
Menu: Tea (including Traidcraft, Earl Grey,
camomile, fruit selection), coffee
(decaffeinated available), hot chocolate (Traidcraft), fruit squashes,
milk, milk shakes, fruit juice, organic orange, apple, lemonade,
Traidcraft cookies, biscuits, Traidcraft geobars, cakes (daily
specials), toasted teacakes. Light lunches available on Fridays.

Started in 2002 in a purpose-built coffee lounge, with easy access, to offer
affordable refreshments, a warm welcome and a caring ministry which
could link community and church.

*Team members learning to work together, a place to meet friends ...
a place to care and listen, to share our faith and to receive from each
other ... Businessmen have noticed the special atmosphere ... facilities
for children and disabled.*

See **What's in a Name?** and **Behind the Scenes**

HAVERHILL

Haverhill Methodist Church
Camps Road
Haverhill
Suffolk

NEXT DOOR

Open: Monday to Friday 10.30 a.m. – 2.30 p.m.
Staff: 24 volunteers
Menu: Tea, coffee, chocolate, soft drinks, cakes, hot/cold sandwiches.
Various salads and savoury pies.

Started in 1993 and attracts over 100 people each day who enjoy cheap
food and drink, the modern décor, welcoming atmosphere and visiting the
bookshop.

*Does more for the community than the church ... Good place to
meet off church premises.*

The building is the renovation of two adjacent cottages next door to the church and 200 yards up the road from the market place.

HELSBY

Helsby Methodist Church
Chester Road
Helsby, Frodsham
Cheshire

THE ROOM COFFEE SHOP

Open: Every day except Wednesday and Sunday 10 a.m. - 1 p.m.
Staff: 3 organisers and 30 volunteers on a rota working approximately one session per month
Menu: Soup, hot drinks (tea, coffee, chocolate), squash and canned drinks, biscuits.

Started in 1997 as an outreach to the village, especially young people. Traidcraft goods, cards, tapes and CDs, books etc. Computer lessons (free) and internet access. Young People's Drop-In Monday evening 7.30 p.m. - 9.30 p.m.

HEREFORD

All Saints Church
High Street
Hereford
HR4 9AA

CAFÉ @ ALL SAINTS

Open: Monday to Saturday 8.30 a.m. - 5.30 p.m.
Staff: 17 full time serving 250-300 daily
Menu: Vegetarian food, fresh produce, assorted teas and coffees. Home-made cakes, wholemeal bread, olive bread rolls, fresh lemonade, full meals.

Started in 1997 when the church was made redundant and going to be boarded up!
The café is different. A modern café in a traditional church ... Warm, friendly, peaceful atmosphere ... Has brought the church to life seven days a week.

See **Change and Renewal**

53

HESWALL

Heswall Methodist Church
Telegraph Road
Heswall
Wirral

THE BEACON

CH60 0AE

Open: Tuesday 10.30 a.m. – 2 p.m., Thursday 10 a.m. – 12 noon,
Friday 10.30 a.m. – 2 p.m., Saturday 10.30 a.m. – 2 p.m.
Staff: 45 volunteers
Menu: Tea, coffee, snacks, lunches (not Saturdays).

Started in 1999 to make use of an empty church house, to build a bridge
to the community, to espouse one-world issues.
*Wonderful development of community and fellowship among
volunteers ... Gathering place for friends ... More awareness of Third
World issues.*

See **Vital Links**

HINCKLEY

St Mary's Church
Church Walk
Hinckley
Leics

ST MARY'S COFFEE BAR

LE10 1OW

Open: Monday to Saturday 10 a.m. – 4 p.m.
Staff: 60 volunteers
Menu: Coffee, tea (both Traidcraft), soft drinks, cup-a-soup,
biscuits, home-made cakes.

Started in 1992 as part of an Open Church Policy in the town
centre.
*Has helped to establish St Mary's as a community
church – growing together as a church and reaching out
into the town ... Friendly ... Stay as long as you
wish ... Cheap cakes ... Women's Institute
Market in the church every Friday ... Ten
per cent of profits to Christian Aid.*

HOLLINSCLOUGH

CHAPEL COMMUNITY HALL

Hollinsclough Methodist Church
Longnor
Near Buxton

Open: May to August Sundays 11 a.m. – 4 p.m. to provide refreshments
and fellowship for travellers
Staff: 3 volunteers
Menu: Hot drinks, cold drinks, sandwiches, home-made cakes,
ice cream, lollipops, biscuits, chocolate and crisps.

Handy stopping-off point for walkers ... Good value for money ...
No objection to muddy boots! ... We have made many new friends
who sometimes travel a distance to our services ... A good fund-
raising source for the chapel.

Hollinsclough is an idyllic hamlet in the Dove Valley. The building now
known as the Chapel Community Hall was once a carpenter's shop. It fell
into disuse and was bought for the chapel for £10
in 1945. Since it was restored ten years ago it
has become a centre for community life
e.g. History Live Group, exhibitions, children's
parties, quiet days, discos and hospitality.

HUDDERSFIELD

MISSION COFFEE BAR

Huddersfield Methodist Mission
Lord Street
Huddersfield
HD1 1QA

Open: Monday to Saturday 9.30 a.m. – 3.30 p.m.
Staff: 20 volunteers
Menu: Tea, coffee, Bovril, milk, minerals. Breakfast (9.30 a.m.
– 11.15 a.m. and 1p.m. – 2.30 p.m.) pork pie (and with
mash and peas) steak and kidney pie (and with mash and peas),
beef dinner, soup, beans on toast, baked potatoes with fillings.
Sandwiches (bacon, beef, ham, cheese, potted beef, dripping).
Toasted teacakes, scones, custard pie, pasty (jam, currant, apple),
vanilla slice, cakes, fresh fruit, yoghurts.

Started in 1980 as a drop-in centre for people shopping in Huddersfield
and also for the lonely and poor.

Friendly, cheap, central, well established ... Meeting place ... adver-
tises our work ... some come to worship as a result.

In the space of thirty years the Mission has moved from Queen Street to King Street to Lord Street (royal connections!) Now in splendid new premises the Coffee Bar is part of the Mission's effort to serve the people of the town centre. The long-established Guild for the Disabled offers a valued meeting point for disabled people and their carers. The Good Enough Project is for adult beginners to learn basic cookery skills. The Welcome Centre helps people in real crisis who are referred by the Benefits Agency. THISISIT (computers for all) is for raw beginners. Counselling Service available for those who need help with a variety of problems.

ILFORD

WELCOME CENTRE

High Road Baptist Church
Ilford
Essex

Open: Tuesday and Thursday 10 a.m. – 3 p.m.
Staff: 2 full time and several volunteers
Menu: Tea, coffee, biscuits, hot three course meal with a vegetarian
option.

Started in 2001 as a drop-in centre particularly to meet the needs of asylum seekers and refugees in the neighbourhood.

Warm welcome, good advice, good food, appreciated by fifty people
a day ... Closer contact with the community ... breaking down
barriers of prejudice ... volunteers from different churches have the
opportunity to work and share together ... At least two people have
become Christians through the work of the Welcome Centre.

The Welcome Centre is based in a brightly decorated former Boys' Brigade hall, which the Baptist Church decided should be used to offer hope, friendship and advice to the neediest members of their community. Three years ago they asked a computer training company using the building to move out. The company donated the furniture to the new centre. Washing machines, showers, cookers and other equipment have been given by other organisations as the centre underwent a £60,000 transformation. Church members raised £35,000 and borrowed the remainder from Churches Together in England and The City Parochial Foundation.

ILKLEY

Christchurch (Methodist / United Reformed)
The Grove
Ilkley, West Yorkshire
LS29 9LW

CHRISTCHURCH COFFEE CENTRE

Open: Monday to Friday 10 a.m. - 4 p.m., Saturday 10 a.m. - 12 noon
Staff: 2 full time (one is a job share) and 60+ volunteers
Menu: Tea, coffee, scones, light refreshments (sandwiches including bacon), toasted sandwiches, soups, beans on toast, jacket potatoes, deserts. Salads in summer.

Started in 1985. A form of outreach following the amalgamation of two churches and the refurbishment of the United Reformed premises on an excellent town centre site. Between 300-400 people a day enjoy good food at reasonable cost, friendly atmosphere and good fellowship.

Has introduced some people to shoppers service and Sunday service. It has enhanced our reputation as an open church offering friendship and access to help in times of stress and need ... It is a well known and well used venue in the town centre.
Any profits provide Christian outreach both locally and overseas. Daily paper, magazines and bookstall available.

KETTERING

Fuller Baptist Church
36 Newland Street
Kettering, Northants
NN16 8JH

FULLER COFFEE HOUSE

Open: Monday to Saturday 10 a.m. - 4.30 p.m.
Staff: 2 full time, 4 part time and 30 volunteers and on Saturdays a team of young people
Menu: Tea, coffee, chocolate, milk shakes, cans of drink, sandwiches, baked potatoes with various fillings, curry, soup and roll, omelettes, bacon and sausage, sandwiches, toasted sandwiches, (no chips).

Started in 1990 when the town centre was redesigned and premises were given to the church in exchange for part of the buildings. The new premises (just around the corner on Newland Street) opened as a Coffee House to extend the mission of the church.

Has given a very active role to a good number of people in the church and other churches to be at the 'coalface' of mission, both directly and indirectly ... Comfortable, good food at reasonable prices and no sense of being rushed.

See **What's in a Name?**

KIMBERLEY

DIFFERENT ASPECTS LTD

Kimberley Baptist Church
Newdigate Street
Kimberley, Nottingham
NG16 2NJ

Open: Monday to Saturday 9 a.m. – 3 p.m.
Staff: 5 part time
Menu: Everything from a toasted teacake to a full roast dinner. All-day full breakfast and small breakfast, hot dishes e.g. chicken nuggets, chips and peas, scampi chips and peas, toasted sandwiches, jacket potatoes, snacks. Beverages include tea, coffee, cappuccino, hot chocolate, fruit juices. There is a children's menu entitled, 'Tasty Meals for Special People': chicken nuggets and chips, egg and chips, sausage and chips, burger and chips, fish fingers and chips. All meals include a drink and a toy or novelty. There are other options including Baby Bowl (a tiny roast dinner for babies or toddlers).

Started in 1991 to bring the church into touch with the local people. The coffee shop also stocks a selection of Christian books and cards as well as toys, CDs and cassettes.

We serve good value meals in a clean friendly environment. People can make friends here or feel comfortable to come alone ... We know many of the 500 a week who come, by their first names ... We are more aware of community needs.

There is always background music and the sharing of faith goes on. An interesting venue for children.

LARKFIELD

Larkfield and East Malling Methodist Church
New Hythe Lane
Larkfield

THE SYCAMORE TREE

Kent

Open: Tuesday to Friday 9.30 a.m. – 12.30 p.m.
Staff: 20 volunteers
Menu: Home-made cake, cheese and beans on toast, soup,
coffee, tea.

Started in 2000 as a response to the New Start initiative for the
Millennium to provide a meeting place for the local community.
*Brought the premises to life ... Created a community resource
for networking ... Volunteers know their regulars and are able
to ask after them ... Child friendly, reasonably priced ... It is
breaking down barriers slowly.*

See **What's in a Name?**

LEEDS

Leeds Methodist Mission
Oxford Place Centre
Leeds

THE LOUNGE

LS1 3AX

Open: Monday to Friday 10 a.m. – 2 p.m.
Staff: 120 volunteers
Menu: (10 a.m. – 12 noon) tea, coffee, orange, cola, milk, scones,
toasted teacakes, biscuits. (12 noon – 2 p.m.) drinks (as above)
plus soup, sandwiches (6 fillings), pork pies, sausage rolls, apple
pie, scones, biscuits, crisps.
Started in 1989 when the church moved into renovated premises and felt
that a café would be a form of outreach to workers and others in the city
centre.
*Our customers (80–100 daily) come from all walks of life. We are
situated next to the Law Courts and the Town Hall and in the
middle of the financial and professional area of the city ... The
volunteers come, not only from our own church, but from churches
throughout the area. Some are people who are not members of any
church, but who wish to do voluntary work ... There is a friendly*

welcoming atmosphere with no pressure to leave quickly and no background music. Our prices are cheaper than other city centre cafés, enabling us to help those who are in need ... The café has contributed to community life in the city. The lunchtime communion service on Wednesdays is supported by people who first came because of the café.

The café is pivotal to the life of this strategically placed city centre church which provides a base for relevant and specific community care e.g. Children Centre for children whose parents are attending the adjacent Courts as defendants, witnesses because of domestic proceedings or to support friends. Open Monday to Friday, supervised by qualified staff. Person to Person open Monday to Friday 10 a.m. - 2 p.m. provides a one-to-one confidential listening service for those in distress or in need of a friend and is staffed by a small ecumenical team of volunteers. It is the only drop-in centre in Leeds where no appointment is necessary and the service is free and accessible to everyone.

LEIGH

COFFEE MORNING

Kingsleigh Methodist Church
Leigh
Lancs

Open: Wednesday, Thursday, Friday 9 a.m. - 12 noon
Saturday 9.30 a.m. - 12 noon
Staff: 35 volunteers
Menu: Tea, coffee, soft drinks, toast, teacakes, crumpets.

Started in 1975 a year after the new church was built in Leigh town centre. Originally it was part of a Special Efforts programme to raise money to purchase furnishings and to provide a working fellowship among members and friends.

It has brought people in from outlying towns and other churches and is a good grapevine for news ... We have come to know about activities in other churches and we support each other.

Between 200 and 250 people a week enjoy meeting friends and making new ones. On Thursdays proceeds are allocated to charities e.g. Methodist Homes, Guide Dogs for the Blind, Cancer Research.

LEIGHTON BUZZARD   All Saints Church
ALL SAINTS CHURCH COFFEE SHOP

Open: Tuesday 10 a.m. – 3.30 p.m., Wednesday 10 a.m. – 2.30 p.m.
        Friday 10 a.m. – 3.30 p.m., Saturday 10 a.m. – 3.30 p.m.
Staff: 30 volunteers serving 700+ each week
Menu: Tea, coffee, hot chocolate, juice, squash, soup, rolls and sand-
        wiches (ham, egg/cress, cheese, tuna, salad) made to order
        freshly. Crisps, chocolate biscuits, home-made cakes and scones.

Started in 1988 to be a pleasant, friendly place for visitors to
the church to have light refreshments; as an informal meeting
place for church members and friends; a service to the wider
community and a possible 'way in' to church for our customers;
a means of income for the church. All the aims met.
*The atmosphere aims to be friendly, 'non churchy' with
cloths and flowers on the tables and attractive china ... The church
has become more a part of the community ... The volunteers are not
all church members ... Part of Leighton Buzzard social life – on
market days very busy ... Some customers baptised/confirmed as a
result of Coffee Shop visits.*

See **Change and Renewal** and **Behind the Scenes**

LISKEARD   **Methodist Church**
                                                   Barn Street
                                                   Liskeard
LISKEARD MANNA   **Cornwall**

Open: Monday to Saturday 10 a.m. – 12.30 p.m.
Staff: 50 volunteers
Menu: Home-made cakes and biscuits, coffee, tea, cans and
        bottled fruit drinks.

Started in 1983 to be a bridge between the street and the church, a sales
outlet for Christian books, greetings cards and Traidcraft items. About
300 people a week (not all at the same time) mix well and friendships are
formed. Whilst the volunteers are mainly from the Liskeard church some
come from other Methodist churches as well as a Roman Catholic and a
Quaker.

Has helped the image of the church in the town and surrounding area. Introduced some people to the church. Among voluntary helpers has given a sense of fulfilment as sharers in the mission of the Servant Church ... Much spontaneous talk and many conversations about faith that go deep ... A meeting place for folk living on their own, some of whom visit several times a week. Supportive calling place for people who help in community concerns. Profits allocated to local and national good causes.

See **What's in a Name?** and **Behind the Scenes**

LIVERPOOL   Bridge Chapel Centre
                                                        Heath Road
                                                         Liverpool
BRIDGE BISTRO   L19 4XR

Open: Monday to Friday 9 a.m. - 4 p.m. (3.30 p.m. Friday)
Staff: 1 full time and 10 volunteers
Menu: Various starters, daily specials, all types of sandwiches, jacket pota-
        toes, toasties, various cakes, coffee, tea, cappuccino, soft drinks.

Started in 2000 as an outreach to the local community and as a con-
venience for the 1,500 people a week who come to the centre which
exercises a caring ministry. 100–150 people a day use the Bistro.
*Food is cheap, well produced and we only deal in portions of 'big'
and 'what's that' size ... Many people meet for lunch, some daily
and a lot of 'Let's meet for lunch' goes on ... We are now accepted
in our local community after initial suspicion ... We invite people
to evangelistic events.*

LIVERPOOL   Frontline Church
                                                     Lawrence Road
                                                         Liverpool
THE FRONT   L15 0FH

Open: Tuesday, Wednesday, Thursday, Friday 10 a.m. - 2 p.m.
Staff: 16 volunteers
Menu: Tea, coffee, all-day breakfasts, toasties. A daily varying board of

five choices at lunchtime. Soup (different every day), roasted red pepper and tomato, golden chicken lasagne, quiche (e.g. leek and cream cheese), baguettes filled with Thai chicken and salad etc.

Started in 1997 to provide a 'front door' to the church and a service to the local community. Some have come through the café into Bible Study groups and to Christian faith. The café is ideally situated at the Crossroads in a densely populated part of Liverpool (Wavertree).

It's warm, friendly and cheap. We serve about 170 meals a day plus beverages ... A focal point for the local community. The café has drawn into fellowship a number who would have been rather marginalised.

LIVERPOOL

STEPPING STONES COFFEE SHOP

Toxteth Tabernacle,
Park Road
Liverpool
L8 6SB

Open: Monday to Friday 9.30 a.m. – 2.30 p.m.
Staff: 2 full time and 12 volunteers
Menu: The easy breakfast: bacon, egg, sausage, baked beans and toast. The big breakfast: two of everything! Plus fried bread, bacon on muffin, black pudding on toast. Tasty baked potatoes; light bites, savoury choice, the bread basket. Something sweet, assorted drinks. There is a special children's menu: fish fingers, chicken nuggets, baby sausages.

Started in 1992 following a neighbourhood survey assessing the peoples priorities. They wanted a café where they could relax and meet. The church responded by seeing it as God's will and a means of reaching out to the neighbourhood with the gospel in a non-threatening way. Gospel tracts are on each table which are read while waiting for meals and taken away.

Cosy, homely. Cost is vital. Food is professionally cooked and presented ... Customers are known by name after a few visits and the staff know their personal tastes before they order ... It is a meeting place for local people and those working in the area. Taxi drivers come regularly ... Prejudice has been broken down, opportunities to witness ... 100 per cent change in perspective of the community towards the church ... A good place for hearing about need and keeping in touch with local situations ... Our church meetings are always better when held here.

LLANDUDNO

St John's Methodist Church
Mostyn Street
Llandudno
LL30 2NN

Open: Tuesday 10 a.m. – 12 noon (summer)
Friday 10 a.m. – 12 noon (all year)
Staff: A rota of volunteers
Menu: Coffee, tea, squash, cakes, Bara-brith.

Started in 1990 as a service to the community, for fund-raising and fellowship. The church is in the centre of this popular holiday resort. There is warm fellowship in a clean hall and excellent toilets. During the summer up to 400 people visit the café over two mornings and in winter about 100 on Fridays.

Communication with holiday makers and the community ... A chance to share the good news and to help people with problems ... The church is open at the same time and on Fridays is staffed by trained Christian listeners ... An opportunity to share with people in their joys and sorrows ... The Tuesday Coffee Mornings are let out to other organisations in the town, e.g. Lifeboat, so giving the church good links with these bodies.

LLANELLI

OCTAGON CAFÉ

Park United Reformed Church
Inikerman Street
Llanelli
SA15 15A

Open: Monday to Friday 9 a.m. – 3.30 p.m.
Staff: 1 full time and 2 volunteers
Menu: Very full breakfast, dinners: pork, beef, chicken, served with stuffing and Yorkshire pudding and five vegetables. Lasagne, curry and rice, faggot dinners with vegetables, jacket potatoes, salads. Pasta

Italiano. Desserts: rice pudding, bread pudding, sponge pudding, custard or ice cream. Snacks and sandwiches available and a variety of hot and cold drinks.

Started in 1997 as a way of the church using its extensive building better and for community use. The community café was always seen as the hub for a range of activities. It progressed from one day open to five days by 1999. The café has attracted community service placements from the Youth Justice Service. The other parts of the project started simultaneously – a workshop for arts and crafts is now thriving, stained glass workshop shared by a branch of Tools for Self Reliance. Local bands use the building for rehearsals and the Youth Theatre performs there. 50 people a day visit the café.

Friendly atmosphere ... it feels like a family ... they can stay as long as they like ... we miss our regular customers when they don't come ... It has brought church and community together, creating a different emphasis in our fellowship together. It has shown the community that the church cares what happens around them.

LOCKERBIE

Lockerbie Salvation Army
15 Station Road
Lockerbie
DG11 2HA

THE COFFEE POT

Open: Daily for meals and snacks
Staff: 3 full time

Located outside the railway station a short distance from the town centre. In a room adjacent to the café is a second-hand clothing store.

See **Change and Renewal**

LONDON
(Opposite British Home Stores)

The Salvation Army
Regent Hall
275 Oxford Street
London, W1C 2OJ

COFFEE SHOP

Open: Monday to Saturday 9.30 a.m. – 4.30 p.m.
Staff: 6 full time serving 1,000 people a week

Menu: Coffees, teas, snacks, baked potatoes, sandwiches, Danish pastries, cakes etc.

 Started in 1997 to extend ministry in London's West End. New people are being reached all the time and this has led to Café Church which began in 2001, one Sunday evening a month. *A new congregation (100–150).*

CAFÉ CHURCH is a new type of service that is interesting and varied as well as relaxed and friendly. It kicks off with coffee at 5.30 p.m. and leads into an exciting programme of worship, including contemporary music, drama, and a message which is relevant to every-day life in the twenty-first century. The menu for 2001 entitled 'A Spiritual Odyssey' included such titles as 'Did Adam and Eve Have Belly Buttons?', 'A Bad Case of Wind!' (Pentecost), 'Jesus Had Smelly Feet!' (on serving others).

REFRESHMENT FOR THE SOUL

The attractive welcome leaflet concludes:
It may be a while since you have been to church, maybe it has never been your thing. Why not come and get a taster, it might be just your cup of tea!

LONDON

MANNA CAFÉ

The Parish of St John and St Peter
Portobello Road
Notting Hill,
London W11 3EB
www.mannafood.com

Open: Tuesday to Saturday 9 a.m. – 5 p.m.
Menu: Breakfast (available until 12 noon) e.g. seasonal fruit salad, Greek yoghurt and honey, organic Muesli, American pancakes, eggs Benedict with crispy bacon or smoked salmon, big bacon sandwich. Lunch (12.30 p.m. – 3 p.m.) soup of the day. Main course with a variety of choices and delicious puddings. Drinks:

expresso, double expresso, cappuccino, hot chocolate, tea (English Breakfast or Earl Grey), herbal tea, cold drinks including seasonal fresh fruit smoothie. A children's menu is available including organic baby food – savoury or sweet.

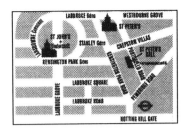

Started in 1995 by the Parish of St John and St Peter as a community outreach.

Has become an important landmark in the local community ... Tourists are delighted to discover it ... The smoothies are delicious.

See **What's in a Name?**

LONDON

Bromley by Bow
United Reformed Church
1 Bruce Road
London, E3 3HN

PIE IN THE SKY

Open: Daily 8 a.m. – 8 p.m.
Staff: 12 full time and 20 volunteers
Menu: Breakfasts, lunches, dinners, snacks, drinks, fruit. Changing daily. e.g. day menu 24 October 2001. Salad bar: spicy peppers, mushrooms and onions, mixed seafood and avocado. Soups: carrot and

parsley or lamb and leek. Main Courses: fish in curry and basil sauce with boiled potatoes and green beans or vegetable parcels with sauté potatoes, salad and spicy sauce. Jacket potatoes: plain with usual fillings or special fillings (sweetcorn, spinach, cheese and cream) Dessert: pear and almond tart with cream.

Started in 1989 when a local woman approached the church and asked if she could realise an ambition to help open a café. It fitted in with other developments e.g. a nursery needing lunches.

Wonderful food at reasonable prices ... High quality surroundings, creative atmosphere, a good place to meet people.

See **What's in a Name?**

LONDON   St Mary-le-Bow Church
                                                        Cheapside
                                                          London
THE PLACE BELOW   EC2V 6AU

Open: Monday to Friday 7.30 a.m. – 3.30 p.m.
Staff: 8 full time
Menu: Fresh food made on the premises. Daily changing menu. 100 per
cent vegetarian.

Started in 1990 to bring more people into the church. Approximately 200
people a day visit the café enjoying good food in a beautiful Norman crypt.

LONDON   Methodist Central Hall
                                                      Storey's Gate
                                                        Westminster
WESLEY'S CAFÉ   SW1H 9NH

Open: Monday to Friday 8 a.m. – 4.30 p.m.
      Saturday and Sunday 9.30 a.m. – 4.30 p.m.
Staff: 6 full time
Menu: A very wide range of refreshments from a cup
of tea or coffee to a three-course meal (hot or
cold).

Started over twenty years ago to provide a focus of hospitality and welcome
at the heart of the capital across the road from Westminster Abbey and the
Houses of Parliament. A modern cafeteria with seating for 200 serving
breakfast, lunch and afternoon tea. Pre-bookable private dining facilities for
groups available at any time. Over a thousand people per week now visit
this affordable, versatile, central London venue which is the flagship of
Methodism.

*It's a very nice, friendly place … A good advert for Methodism and
Christianity.*
The top picture on the back cover of this book is of Wesley's Café at
Central Hall.
See **What's in a Name?**

MALVERN

The Lyttelton Well Ltd
Church Street
Malvern, Worcs
THE LYTTELTON WELL
WR14 2AY

Open: Monday to Saturday 10 a.m. - 5 p.m.
Staff: Over 100 volunteers
Menu: Coffee and decaffeinated coffee, tea (including
Indian, decaffeinated, Earl Grey or herbal), hot
chocolate. A variety of cold drinks, toast,
toasted teacake, scone, two scones with jam and
Cornish clotted cream and a pot of tea. (11.30 a.m. - 3.30 p.m.)
soup of the day with roll and butter, baked potato (variety of
fillings and salad garnish). Sandwiches (variety of fillings with
salad garnish). On toast (poached eggs, mushrooms, baked beans,
spaghetti hoops), ploughman's, salads.

Started in 1993 when Christians in Malvern felt the need to have a street
front venture in which to witness to their faith. The café seats 27 and is
rarely empty.

*Good atmosphere, good home-made food, caring and friendly staff
... The Well is jointly run by fifteen churches in Malvern and has
shown that Christians can work together ... Many lonely people have
found caring and friendship through the Well.*

See **Churches Working Together** and **Behind the Scenes**

MANCHESTER

Manchester Methodist Centre
Central Hall, Oldham Street
Manchester
CAFÉ CENTRAL
M1 1JT

Open: Tuesday 11 a.m. - 2 p.m.
Staff: 5 volunteers
Menu: Tea, coffee, hot chocolate, cans, sandwiches, toasties, jacket
potatoes, pork pies, toast, beans on toast, toasted teacakes, cakes,
biscuits, scones.

Started during Lent 2000 (a positive Lent!) Proved to be so successful it has
continued attracting 50 to 60 people each week.

We have quite a few shoppers coming in who ask questions, e.g. Are you a church? ... Food is reasonably priced and served in a quiet friendly atmosphere ... Income raised donated to NCH and other charities.

The café is also a meeting place for those attending the Tuesday midday service at 12.45 p.m. During the Commonwealth Games Café Central was open early till late. There is a prayer chapel for quiet reflection. 'Befrienders' – a listening and practical support service – is available Monday to Friday, 2 p.m. to 4 p.m. Formerly part of the Manchester and Salford Mission Circuit (now Manchester Central).

* In 1899 the Mission opened a women's night shelter and training home in Great Ancoats Street. On the ground floor was a **Coffee** * **Tavern**.

MARKET HARBOROUGH

NEW HORIZONS

Market Harborough Baptist Church
Manor Walk
Market Harborough
Leicestershire

Open: Monday to Friday 9.45 a.m. – 4 p.m.
Staff: 3 part time and 35 volunteers
Menu: Hot and cold drinks, scones, teacakes, pastries, jacket potatoes, toasted sandwiches, salads, daily hot specials (lunches).

Started in 1991.

As a town centre church we had a desire to reach out into the community ... Many contacts with the local community. A large number of people use the café daily and recommend New Horizons to friends ... We have 40 table settings and the café is full on most days, especially early morning and lunchtimes are very busy ... Warm friendly welcome ... quality food ... value for money.

MATLOCK

FRIDAY LUNCH

Methodist / United Reformed Church
Bank Road, Matlock
Derbyshire

Open: Friday 12 noon – 1.30 p.m.
Staff: 32 volunteers (monthly rota)
Menu: 3 course meal (tea or coffee free). No charge.
Recommended a minimum of £1 per course
donation.

Started in 1996 as an extension of Lent Lunches and outreach to the community. Now a firm fixture in the life of a church where the premises have been redeveloped in recent years. A wonderfully spacious kitchen. About 70 people attend the Friday Lunches.

Good Food and Fellowship ... Many friendships have been formed between voluntary workers and visitors ... The building has become more familiar to many people. They feel at home ... Established the church as a centre for the local community to meet in an informal setting ... Has raised many thousands of pounds not only for church funds (during the redevelopment) but for many other good causes.

NELSON

COFFEE LOUNGE

Central Methodist Church
Car Road
Nelson, Lancs

Open: Monday to Saturday 10 a.m. – 4 p.m.
Staff: 18 volunteers
Menu: Snacks (apart from Friday), a traditional range of sandwiches are served at lunchtime.

Started in 1991 in response to a need expressed by older people. Approximately 25 people a day pass through but Wednesday and Friday, shopping days in town, are the busiest.

Homely, comfortable, inexpensive ... chance to meet with friends ... very ecumenical.

There is a Development Scheme planned for this year and in the new premises the Coffee Lounge will be on the front instead of tucked away as it is at present.

New Malden Methodist Church
49 High Street
New Malden, Surrey
KT3 4BY

THE WELCOME AREA

Open: Monday to Friday 10 a.m. – 2 p.m., Saturday 10 a.m. – 12 noon
Staff: 60 volunteers working in twos for a two-hour shift
Menu: Coffee, tea, hot chocolate, squash, milk, soft drinks, biscuits, flapjacks.

Started because this church is in the High Street and has now taken full advantage of its position by opening up the front of the church with welcoming glass doors.

Friendly, bright, comfortable. All ages come ... New friendships are made ... Team spirit ... A caring ministry ... Much greater contact with the community ... We invite people to bring their own sandwiches, especially office workers.

The morning session (10 a.m. to 12 noon) enables those who shop to have coffee/tea etc. The lunchtime hours enable those who work in New Malden to also use the facility. The welcome area leads into the church enabling anyone to use the church for prayer or quiet.

The volunteers understand the ethos of the church. That is, we are available to provide hospitality and welcome. We will witness to our faith, but with sensitivity and care. We respect the personal boundaries of those visiting. Many will ask questions. We will answer on behalf of all the churches in the area.

A bookshop, play area, the sanctuary and toilets with baby changing facilities are available from the welcome area. Any profit from the project is directed to an overseas and home charity on an annual basis. The Church Council decides in advance who the church will support. An approximate £5,000 was sent last year in total. Since staff give their time free, it enables the church to be generous in this way. Staff would also speak of the way in which they have discovered a broader ministry to the community. The number of contacts per week with different people is enormous. People from the community also become aware that the church is available and open and can be used in a number of ways apart from offering worship. This all helps the profile of the church and building bridges and encouraging confidence.

NEWCASTLE

Brunswick Methodist Church
Brunswick Place
Newcastle upon Tyne
NE1 7BI

BRUNSWICK SANDWICH BAR

Open: Monday to Friday 11.15 a.m. – 1.15 p.m.
Saturday 10 a.m. – 12 noon
Staff: 40 volunteers
Menu: Tea, coffee, scones, chocolate, biscuits,
bread buns with a range of fillings (bread
buns are Geordie sandwiches in a whole
range of mouth-watering fillings and at very
competitive prices!), cheese and biscuits.

Started in 1981 as an outreach ministry in the city centre, an avenue of
community service and a fund-raiser. Catering for 1,000 people a week it
is very widely known and popular.

Clean, cheerful premises, cheap high quality food fresh each day,
welcoming staff ... Widely appreciated by many visitors to the city ...
Brings people in, breaks the ice, gives opportunity for conversation.
Customers often use the Prayer Chapel or Listening Post.

See **Vital Links**

NEWMARKET

Christchurch Methodist / United Reformed Church
65 High Street, Newmarket
Suffolk CB8 8NA

THE STABLE

Open: Tuesday 9 a.m. – 2 p.m., Thursday 9 a.m. – 1 p.m.
Friday 9 a.m. – 1 p.m., Saturday 9 a.m. – 1 p.m.
(Teens Bar Friday 7 p.m. – 10 p.m. Non-alcoholic bar and
games room)
Staff: 5 part time and 32 volunteers
Menu: Coffee (filter and instant), tea (pot or cup), hot chocolate, fruit
juice and other cold drinks, milk shakes. Home-made soup with
bread roll. Sandwiches and rolls (variety of fillings), toast and
toasted sandwiches, egg, cheese or beans on toast, jacket potatoes
(a variety of fillings), breakfasts, light lunches, quiche, omelettes,
specials each day e.g. lasagne, pasta, broccoli bake.

Started in 1994 when the United Reformed Church amalgamated with Christchurch Methodist Church. In consultation with other churches and organisations it was felt that the town needed a meeting place where everyone could feel included. The former United Reformed Church premises on the High Street were adapted for this purpose. Now over 500 people a week visit the café.

Heightened awareness within the local community ... Informality, friendly people, non-judgmental, offering continuity in people's lives ... Dignity, discretion, comfort – no one need feel alone ... A central focus.

See **What's in a Name?** and **Behind the Scenes**

NORTH WALSHAM

North Walsham Methodist Church
18 Market Street
North Walsham
THE CARPENTER'S ARMS
Norfolk

Open: Monday, Thursday and Saturday 10 a.m. - 2 p.m.
Tuesday 4.30 p.m. - 6 p.m., Wednesday 2 p.m. - 4.30 p.m.
Staff: 24 volunteers
Menu: Cans of soft drinks, sweets, biscuits, chips, burgers, sandwiches, toasted sandwiches, noodles, tea, coffee, squash.

Started in 1995 to meet the needs of local young people. About 40 come each time the café is open.

Helps clear the streets and gives youngsters, especially the disaffected, a place to go.

NORTHAMPTON

Northampton Emmanuel Church
Weston Favell Centre
Billingbrook Road
Northampton
EMMANUEL CHURCH COFFEE SHOP
NN3 8JR

Open: Monday to Friday 10 a.m. - 2 p.m., Saturday 10 a.m. - 12 noon
Staff: 3 full time and 20 volunteers
Menu: Coffee, chocolate, Bovril, tea, cold drinks. Cooked breakfast, 5 or

7 items, freshly baked baguettes (various fillings), toasties, omelettes, jacket potatoes (various fillings), light snacks, sandwiches and rolls, a selection of home-made cakes.

Started in 1976. Purpose built as part of new church development on the Eastern District of Northampton – a London overspill project.

Friendly, reasonable prices, stay as long as you like. Welcoming to disabled and disadvantaged groups. Some come every day ... A place where people can come to meet God and each other ... A focal point for caring agencies in a busy shopping centre ... About 150 people each day visit the café so it is self supporting and keeps the building open for other activities ... It is a significant part of the weekday church.

NOTTINGHAM

WESLEY'S LIFE AT THE CENTRE

Nottingham Methodist Mission
22 Lower Parliament Street
Nottingham
NG1 3DA

Open: Monday to Saturday 10 a.m. – 2.30 p.m.
Staff: 40 volunteers
Menu: Wide selection of hot and cold drinks, sandwiches, toasted sandwiches, selection of toppings on toast, jacket potatoes and salads, cakes, scones, teacakes, biscuits.

Started in 1989 following redevelopment of the city centre premises. About 200 people a day visit the café.

Wesley's is one of our main areas of outreach into the city centre. Many people have joined fellowship groups and started to attend worship after visiting Wesley's ... Cheerful, friendly staff ... very pleasant surroundings ... good wholesome food at reasonable prices ... can always find someone to talk to and children find playmates.

A volunteer's name badge

See **What's in a Name?**

OLD BASING   St Mary's Parish Church
                                                              Old Basing
                                                       Basingstoke, Hants
LE CAFÉ BIENVENU   RG24 8WE

Open: Friday 8.45 a.m. – 11 a.m. (school term time only)
Staff: 15 volunteers
Menu: Coffee, tea, hot chocolate, pain au choclat, croissants, juice,
biscuits (except Red Nose Day when it's 'bacon butties').

Started in 1998 in response to a need for mothers to meet and make
friends. Between 10 and 40 attend.
*They can relax and meet others in a safe friendly environment ... lots
of new friendships formed.*
A way of supporting Mums who may feel isolated.

*It has shown non-churchgoers a friendly,
fun side of church and helped them to feel
that they can belong ... Some of the 'regulars' have now formed a discussion group*
Regular donations to a variety of charities and
church.

See **Vital Links** and **Behind the Scenes**

OLDHAM METHODIST CIRCUIT   Church Lane
                                                               Oldham
                                                             OL1 3AR
THE SALT CELLAR   www.saltcellar.org.uk

Open: Monday to Saturday 10 a.m. – 4 p.m.
Staff: 2 full time, 19 part time and 150 volunteers
Menu: Breakfast served until 11 a.m. small, large, Full
Monty (bacon, egg sausage, beans, tomato, black
pudding, mushrooms, with extras of everything!)
Snacks on toast including baked beans, cheese, egg, tomatoes.
Lighter snacks including crumpets and toasted teacakes. Main
courses: soup of the day, quiche, cottage pie, and steak and kidney
pie with vegetables. Daily specials, jacket potatoes with a variety of
fillings and salad garnish. Salads, sandwiches, take-aways. An

amazing variety of cakes and sweets, fresh fruit. Tea, coffee (including specialities), hot chocolate, Horlicks, milk shakes, fruit drinks. A children's menu is available called Noah's with Ark Spuds (jacket potato with filling, egg mayonnaise, tuna or beans); Mrs Noah's Picnic Lunch (ham, cheese or tuna sandwich, orange squash or small pop, Penguin biscuit); Shem-ham big dinner (sausage and beans on toast); Mr Noah's treats on toast (animal spaghetti or beans); milk shakes, rainbow ice cream, Penguin biscuits.

Started in 1991 to provide in the town centre a non-threatening meeting point for Christians, people of other faiths and those with no faith at all. Also to provide the area with access to Christian resources: books, magazines, cards, videos etc.

Offers a place of welcome, safety and compassion to 3,000 people a week.

See **Change and Renewal**

PADIHAM   Padiham Methodist Church
                                                                  Burnley
WESLEY CENTRE COFFEE BAR   Lancs

Open: Tuesday, Wednesday, Thursday, Friday 9.30 a.m. – 1.30 p.m.
Staff: 2 full time and 14 volunteers
Menu: (Morning) toast, bacon sandwiches etc. (Lunches) pies, quiches, salad, soup, sandwiches, cheese/beans on toast, fruit pies, trifles etc.

Started in 1992 when the church converted a Working Men's Club into a worship centre and rooms for community use.

It's a large one storey building in the centre of town which immediately spoke to us as being ideal to incorporate a coffee bar to bring the community into the church building ... Situated almost opposite the Medical Centre it has proved beneficial to people for whom medical personnel do not have time to listen. Many bereaved people have come in, lonely and depressed, and found help ... Some people regard it as a lifeline and almost as their church ... It is used to bring community groups together.

PENMAENMAWR

Christian Bookshop and Tea Room
1 Westminster Buildings
Penmaenmawr
North Wales LL34 6BY

THE OASIS

Open: Monday to Friday (except Bank Holidays)
Staff: 1 manager, 2 assistants
Menu: Light snacks, hot and cold drinks, soups and broth, various toppings on toast, toasted teacakes, scones with butter, jam and cream, cakes and gateaux.

Started in 1994 as a Christian ministry in the area and among tourists. *Has given us an outreach opportunity in the main village street next door to the Post Office ... Has fostered close links between the churches.*

PENRHYS RHONDDA

Local Ecumenical Partnership
Heol Y Waun
Penrhys Rhondda
Cynon Taf
CF43 3NW

LLANFAIR CAFÉ

Open: Tuesday to Friday 9 a.m. - 2 p.m.
Staff: 10 volunteers plus 4 overseas volunteers per year
Menu: Sandwiches, rolls, things on toast, breakfasts, salads, omelettes, baked potatoes, special Gladys sandwich, tea, coffee (Fairtrade), soft drinks, milk shakes. A wide selection of 1p sweets available.

Started in 1991 as a result of the church re-assessing its role and asking the community how it could better serve it. The café is one of several projects including a launderette, a 'nearly new' shop, a homework club and music room. The evening café is geared towards children and young people but adults are encouraged to mix with them and play games, cards, dominoes etc.

The church is no longer seen as an alien institution ... the café and projects have enabled us to be close to the community and to share its pain and happiness ... Colourful children's work, Christian Aid and Traidcraft posters, justice issues, thought-provoking sayings are displayed on the walls and questions lead to conversation.

Maybe all this has stimulated a community of 1,000 people to raise £2,000 during the last Christian Aid Week.

PLYMOUTH

Plymouth Methodist Central Hall
Eastlake Street
Plymouth
PL1 1B

DISCOVERY CAFÉ

Open: Monday to Saturday 10 a.m. – 3 p.m.
Staff: 8 full time and 25 volunteers serving 120–150 each day
Menu: Main hot meals include ham, egg and chips, scampi and chips, cottage/steak and kidney/ chicken and mushroom pies or vegetarian burger with garnish or chips, also meal of the day at special prices. Big breakfasts served from 10 a.m. – 1.30 p.m. including egg, bacon, sausage, waffle, tomato, baked beans, toast, marmalade and tea. Snacks: soup and bread, jacket potato with choice of filling, filled rolls, sandwiches, quiche; cakes and desserts and children's meals, plus a variety of drinks. Group bookings are welcome for breakfasts, lunches or teas.

Started in 1997 to extend the work already started in a smaller version of the café of bridging the gap between church and community.
Peaceful, clean, friendly ... Freshly cooked food, children's menu available, high chairs and a fenced play area, easy access for prams and wheel chairs, baby feeding/changing room, toilets ... It has provided a setting for fellowship within the church, the sharing of gifts and in-depth conversations ... Many people in Plymouth and around consider it a safe, reliable place to meet and eat ... You are welcome - no matter how little or how much money or time you spend.
See **What's in a Name?**

PORTSMOUTH   Citadel Corps of the Salvation Army
                                                              22-24 Lake Road
                                                                   Portsmouth
                                                                        Hants
THE HAVEN   PO1 4HA

Open: Monday to Saturday 9 a.m. – 2.30 p.m.
Staff: 3 full time and 4-10 volunteers serving 100 people
        per day
Menu: One main meal option (2 courses), all day
        breakfast, variety of cooked meals and snacks.

Started in 1994 as part of The Haven Community Centre.
*Good setting, warm friendly atmosphere, good food at very reason-
able prices ... Increased fellowship, widened contacts in the community. Awareness of local people and their needs.*
As part of the overall ministry of The Haven it is invaluable.

See **Vital Links**

PORTSMOUTH   Wesley Methodist Centre
                                                          Fratton Road
WESLEY COFFEE BAR   Portsmouth

Open: Tuesday to Friday 9.30 a.m. – 12 noon
Staff: 6 volunteers
Menu: Tea, coffee, Bovril, drinking chocolate, squash, toast with
        marmalade or jam, toasted teacakes, biscuits.

Started in the 1960s when the church was known as Portsmouth Central
Hall and re-opened in a purpose-built coffee bar area when the new Wesley
Centre was built in 1991. On a main road in a busy area of the city, the
coffee area is clearly visible to passers by.
*Friendliness – volunteers are always willing to lend a listening ear ...
People living on their own like to come in for a chat ... The Centre
is used for a variety of meetings and the Coffee Bar is a good drop-
in spot before or after.*

POYNTON

BAPTIST CHURCH

Poynton Baptist Church
Park Lane
Poynton, Cheshire
SK12 1RE

Open: Tuesday, Thursday, Saturday 10 a.m. - 12 noon
Staff: 8 volunteers
Menu: Coffee, tea, orange, biscuits.

Started in 1996 to make contacts within the community. About 30 people a day are given the opportunity to get to know each other.

POYNTON METHODIST CHURCH

OPEN HANDS

Civic Hall Car Park
Poynton
Cheshire
SK12 1RB

Open: Monday to Friday 10 a.m. - 12 noon
Staff: 1 part time, 77 volunteers (including, office, driving, coffee)
Menu: Tea, coffee, orange juice, biscuits.

Started in 1981 for the benefit of people seeking help. Open Hands is more than a coffee shop. The comfortable coffee area is however, the first impression given to the visitor who walks through the door.

Some workmen in the area have been delighted to find our service ... Some regular customers see this as a lifeline and cannot imagine what they would do if we weren't here.

The other part of the project involves volunteer drivers providing a service to those unable to use public transport. Last year 323 people were helped and 1,079 journeys made - shopping, hospital/medical centre appointments and visiting relatives in hospital being the most frequent requests made.

PRESTON
THE OLIVE GROVE

Lune Street Methodist Church
Preston

Open: Monday to Saturday 10.30 a.m. - 1 p.m.
(closing earlier on Wednesday and Saturday)
Staff: 25 volunteers

Menu: Coffee, tea, hot chocolate, milk, orange juice, Ribena, biscuits, home-made cakes, toasted teacakes, mince pies (seasonal).

Started in the 1960s in schoolroom in church basement. Moved into extensive and refurbished church foyer in 1980s. The schoolroom has now been converted into a soup kitchen and shelter for the homeless.

Premises open daily bringing people into the building which has undergone extensive repairs through café income ... Families welcome – children can play in the crèche. Bright, cheerful and friendly with very reasonable prices ... Opportunity to sit quietly and prayerfully in church and put a written prayer on the prayer tree ... A meeting point for over 400 people who sometimes meet several times a week ... Staff become closer and are always willing to listen to each other. They share difficulties and confidences with those they serve.

SCARBOROUGH

WESTBOROUGH COFFEE LOUNGE

Westborough Methodist Church
Scarborough
YO11 6UH

Open: Tuesday to Friday
Staff: 52 volunteers
Menu: Light snacks (scone with butter and jam, toasted teacakes and a selection of desserts). Lunchtime snacks (soup with roll and butter, ham, tuna or cheese sandwich, open roll with choice of fillings and salad trim, jacket potatoes, salads, toasted sandwiches, quiche – all with salad trim).

Started in the mid-1990s when the church was redeveloped and now catering for an average through the year of over 100 people a day.

Good ambience, we have a large airy space which looks good ... Cheap, tasty and pleasantly presented food ... The church is now an every-day church, opened up to many who would not normally ever enter a church ... It has enhanced the family life of the church and given a purpose to many of the volunteers. New friendships formed among staff and customers.

Sheffield Methodist Mission
Victoria Hall
Norfolk Street
Sheffield S1 2JB

CITY CENTRE COFFEE

Open: Monday to Saturday 10 a.m. to 12 noon
Staff: 30 volunteers
Menu: Coffee, tea, fruit, squash, biscuits, cakes.

Started in 1966 on Fridays and Saturdays, but since the early 1980s has operated each day as an extension of the church's ministry to the city centre. Over 1,000 people come in a week and they appreciate the relaxed atmosphere in which they can leisurely meet friends or simply spend time alone. Very low charges are made and members of staff are always available to discuss pastoral problems.

Some customers now attend the Thursday lunchtime worship ... Good fellowship among volunteer staff and wonderful friendship among regular customers.

The minister is involved in several hours of pastoral conversations each week and people know that he will sign passport forms and other such documents. Joys are shared e.g. birthdays, wedding anniversaries etc. Open from 8 a.m. – 9.30 p.m. the Victoria Hall is a seven-day-a-week church, responding to the social needs of the city centre. In addition to City Centre Coffee, served daily, distribution of clothing, free of charge, to the homeless and to all referred by Social Services, the Probation Service and Police, is a feature of our work. The Victoria Hall is the city centre venue for 84 organisations which regularly use the building. Sheffield's Refugee and Asylum Seekers' Drop-In is held on the premises. As a gathered congregation the church retains its worshipping heart, holding services not only in English, but catering for a French-speaking, mainly African, ecumenical congregation. The Victoria Hall is used by the Methodist Church at District and Connexional levels and by the Anglican and Roman Catholic Churches for special occasions.

Sheffield Inner City Ecumenical Mission
199 Verdon Street
Sheffield
S3 9QQ

THE FURNIVAL CAFÉ

Open: Tuesday to Friday 10 a.m. - 3 p.m.
Staff: 1 full-time catering manager and 8 volunteers
Menu: Specials, lasagne, home-made pies, baked potatoes, chips, cakes, puddings, tarts, scones, flapjack, quiche, all-day breakfast, toast, tea, coffee, squash.

Started in 1997 in direct and specific response to the expressed needs of local people. The Furnival was, until 1996, a public house. It is now a church and community centre with the café at the hub of its life. There is a play area for children and the old pub cellar has been converted into an informal place for young people excluded from school. There is also a launderette and three shops next to the Furnival are now meeting community needs for second-hand clothes, help and information and the Healthy Housing Initiative.
Reflects the language of the locality ... exercises a respect for all policy ... user friendly, tolerant of difference.

SHEFFIELD

Sheffield Central United Reformed Church
60 Norfolk Street
Sheffield
S1 2JB

JUST SERVING

Open: Tuesday 10.30 a.m. - 1 p.m.
(there are also coffee mornings held on Friday and Saturday)
Staff: 40 volunteers
Menu: Toasted teacakes, sandwiches (cheese, tuna, egg, corned beef), sausage rolls, custards, pastries, fruit pies, tea, coffee, soft drinks.

Started in 1970 when the new church was built to serve the city centre. People were sitting on walls or the church steps to eat their sandwiches at lunchtime. They valued the invitation to step inside for drinks and then, by popular demand, soup, sandwiches, and deserts. Up to 500 people were served some days. During the European Football Championships in 1996 a café operated called The Corner Flag Café with tables and chairs extending from a downstairs room to a pavement outside. Many local artists displayed and sold their paintings. There is at present a redevelopment scheme of the outside of the church to provide easier access and a welcoming front entrance. This may lead to an extension of the church's hospitality programme.

SHIPLEY

CUPPACARE

Churches Together in Shipley
c/o Shipley Baptist Church
New Kirkgate, Shipley
West Yorkshire

Open: Monday and Friday 10 a.m. - 1.30 p.m.
(except end of July to early September,
2 weeks at Christmas and 2 weeks at Easter)
Staff: 30 volunteers. Those on duty join for Bible reading and prayer at
9.45 a.m. - customers' requests for prayer are included
Menu: Filled rolls, soup, scones, biscuits, tea, coffee, orange drinks.

Started in 1986 to provide a town centre drop-in Christian café for the general public as a means of evangelism and fellowship which included Christian literature.

There's always a good 'buzz'; waitress service to the tables; ample portions of food at minimal prices; a good range of denominations represented. Elderly people have easy access from the town centre. Homeless people are given free food and drink ... Members of smaller churches appreciate this means of fellowship during the week ... Our slogan is 'We're not fund-raising, we're faith-raising'.

See **Churches Working Together**

SOLIHULL

THE OCTAGON COFFEE SHOP

Shirley Methodist Church
Stratford Road
Shirley, Solihull
Birmingham
www.shirleymethodist.org.uk

Open: Monday to Saturday 10 a.m. - 2.30 p.m.
Staff: 130 volunteers

Menu: Coffee, tea, hot chocolate, cold drinks, teacakes, toast, sandwiches, baked potatoes, Cornish pasties, toasted sandwiches, cakes, biscuits, crisps.

Started in 1993 as a community outreach from a new church building and now attracting about a thousand people a week.

What people have been looking for, some come every day. Good coffee, friendly welcome, fellowship of church improved 100 per cent. Has made a great difference to church finances and brought new people into the church.

SOUTHPORT

COFFEE SHOP

Salvation Army
61 Shakespeare Street
Southport
Merseyside

Open: Monday to Friday 10 a.m. - 1 p.m.
Staff: 1 full time and 30 volunteers
Menu: High quality, low cost savoury and sweet snacks and drinks.

Started in 1992 to provide a drop-in centre for the local community where a listening ear would be available. 40-50 come per day, some while visiting the Salvation Army clubs / charity shop / warehouse.

Meeting place for members who know each other better through visiting the café or working there ... useful in advertising Salvation Army events ... has given us a much higher profile in the town ... The cost and quality of food is appreciated and the friendly helpful staff ... There is an increased appreciation of the Salvation Army's commitment to the community.

STAFFORD

COFFEE BAR

Trinity Church (Methodist/United Reformed)
Mount Street
Stafford

Open: Monday, Wednesday, Thursday 10 a.m. - 12.45 p.m.
Tuesday and Friday 10 a.m. - 1.45 p.m.
Staff: 38 volunteers

Menu: (Monday) tea, coffee, squash, milk. (Tuesday and Friday) drinks, as above, soup, rolls with a variety of fillings, scones, buns. (Wednesday) drinks, as above, plus hot chocolate and buttered toast. (Thursday) drinks, as above, plus buns and scones. All drinks are served with two complementary biscuits. Nothing on the menu costs more than 40p.

Started in the 1980s when the church was built as a joint URC/Methodist venture to provide a town centre service and witness as part of the outreach of the church.

We aim to provide a warm friendly welcome in comfortable surroundings ... The place is unhurried and the staff try to lend a listening ear and practical help.

Each session starts with the volunteers on duty sharing in a fellowship of prayer. Daily prayers are held in church at 11 a.m. and on Thursdays at the same time there is a service of Holy Communion. The town centre position of the church in the shopping area gives it good visibility and about 700 people a week visit. Groups of children from a nearby Special School and adults from a Training Centre use the coffee bar as a socialising centre. Two girls from the Centre work on the volunteers' rota.

St Ives   St Ives Free Church
                                                 Market Hill
                                                     St Ives
Tookey's Coffee Shop   Cambs

Open: Monday to Friday 9.30 a.m. - 2 p.m.,
        Saturday 9.30 a.m. - 4 p.m.
Staff: All volunteers serving 250–300 on Mondays and 50 per day
        Tuesday to Saturday
Menu: Sandwiches, bacon and egg rolls, toasted teacakes, home-baked
        fruit and cheese scones. Full range of confectionary. Tea, coffee,
        cold drinks.

Started in 1995 when a ground floor area in this large church in the market place of St Ives was transformed into a café/bookshop and Traidcraft outlet.

Good food, great scones, friendly service, time to sit and feel at home as long as you like ... The accessibility is excellent and the town centre location ... Very busy on Monday (market day) when the church hall is used.

See **What's in a Name?**

SWANSEA

Christwell United Reformed Church
Manselton Road
Manselton

CHRISTWELL COFFEE SHOP

Swansea

Open: Tuesday, Wednesday, Thursday 10.30 a.m. - 1 p.m.
Staff: 1 full time and 8 volunteers
Menu: Tea, coffee, cans and cartons of soft drinks, biscuits, toast, beans, cheese, egg on toast, bacon sandwich roll, chips with beans, bacon, egg, sausage, ham. Brunch (3 items on toast), omelettes (plain, cheese, with salad), jacket potatoes with choice of fillings, ham salad, cheese salad, home-made soup and roll, cup-a-soup, cakes.

Started in 1999 to serve the community and church members. About 30 people a day enjoy a drink and chat. 20 enjoy dinner daily plus the Parent and Toddler Group and other educational groups.

It has shown us how to be a family in God's House ... We are learning to spread God's love. The opportunity to talk about every-day events, to share concerns and to help each other in any ways possible.

WALSALL

St Paul's Church
Darwall Street
Walsall, West Midlands

THE CROSSING COFFEE SHOP

WS1 1DA

Open: Monday to Friday 9 a.m. - 4 p.m., Saturday 9 a.m. - 5 p.m.
Staff: 15 (mostly part time)
Menu: Beverages: tea including fruit, herbal, speciality; coffee including cappuccino-style coffee or 'frothy' coffee; hot chocolate, milk and

cold drinks. To get you started, full English breakfast available until 11.30 a.m. Toast and the like, and toasties. Omelettes (farmhouse cheese, mushrooms, ham, chicken). Sandwiches with a variety of fifteen fillings. Jacket potatoes with fourteen different fillings. Lite bites – soup, Yorkshire pudding with filling of the day. Farmhouse pâté with mango chutney served with hot buttered toast. Two warm croissants with ham, melted cheese and salad garnish. Sweet tooth: doughnuts, custard tarts, bread pudding, rock cakes, scones, home-made cake. There is a specials board each day and smaller half portions from the menu at half price for children plus cheese and tomato pizza.

Started in 1996 as part of the redevelopment of the church which included offices and shops. Caters for 220 people a day.

Relaxed environment ... Pleasant ... Healthy eating ... Some private seating ... Increased awareness and evangelical opportunities ... It has brought people in who would otherwise not enter a church building and gives a good impression. There is always church information around and easy access to clergy.

See **Change and Renewal**

Central Hall Methodist Church
                                                        Ablewell Street
The Meeting Place   Walsall WS1

Open: Friday 10.30 a.m. – 2 p.m., Saturday 10.30 a.m. – 1 p.m.
Staff: 20 volunteers
Menu: Tea, coffee, squash, cakes, biscuits.

Started in 1997 to raise the profile of the church at street level and as a means of outreach to the local community. Provides an opportunity for 20-40 people a day to chat in a relaxed atmosphere. New links with passers-by and with local shopkeepers – Orthodox and Hindu etc. The local church fellowship has been strengthened through the café.

WARWICK

Castle Hill Baptist Church
Castle Hill
Warwick

MEETING POINT

Open: Tuesday to Saturday 10.30 a.m. - 4.30 p.m.
Staff: 25–30 volunteers
Menu: A variety of soft drinks, cans, squash, milk shakes, tea, coffee, hot chocolate, various teas and coffee. On-toast snacks, teacakes, scones, sandwiches, baps with a variety of fillings, both hot and cold. Cooked breakfast. Freshly made soup of the day and every day a different special. A selection of sweets.

Started in 1992 as an outreach to local people and tourists. Depending on the season and weather the café can expect between 45 and 150 customers a day.

They like the quiet unhurried atmosphere and that it is light and bright ... Something different ... It is a point of contact for people who may be wary of the more formal aspect of the main building ... People introduced to the church through the café.

Traidcraft promoted.

WARWICK

St Michael's Church
3 Slade Hill
Hampton Magna
Warwick
CV35 8SA

THE OPEN DOOR FAIR TRADE SHOP AND CAFÉ

Open: Monday to Saturday 9 a.m. - 5 p.m.
Staff: 2 full time and 6 volunteers
Menu: Fairtrade beverages (filter coffee, cappuccino, decaffeinated coffee), hot chocolate, tea (African Gold, Assam, Earl Grey, Indian Ocean), cold drinks, sandwiches, jacket potatoes, toasties, soup, home-made cakes and apple pie. A super children's menu is

90

available with a range of choices: 'A Flying Ted Special' (sandwich, crisps, pudding, panda pop, squash or milk), 'Lion's Lunch Time Special' (toast topper and as above). There is a Taste and See Take-Away Service and a Taste and See Buffet Service. All prices include a five per cent fair-trade premium. This donation is given to Third World projects.

Started in 1999 to bring the church into the heart of the community by providing a meeting and eating place in the shopping centre and to promote Fairtrade food and goods and awareness of fair trade issues. Every day starts with a fifteen minute prayer time at 8.45 a.m. when prayers are said for people, organisations, community and world concerns.

Welcoming and friendly atmosphere ... Bright and cheerful surroundings ... Good food, well prepared ... Friendly staff who have a listening ear ... Meeting point for friends ... Opportunity to develop links with people and organisations ... To extend the mission of the church in serving the community and promoting issues of fair trade and justice and reconciliation ... Provides support to people in time of need – bereavement, loneliness – someone to talk to ... Opportunity to draw alongside people and answer questions about faith in a natural, relaxed way ... Youth group meets regularly each month.

WARWICK

THE ROCK

Christ Church Coffee Shop
Woodloes Park
Warwick
CV34 5RN

Open: Monday 9 a.m. – 12 noon
Tuesday, Wednesday and Thursday 9 a.m. – 1.30 p.m.
Friday 9 a.m. – 12 noon, Saturday 10 a.m. – 12 noon
Staff: 25 volunteers serving 2-20 each day (varies considerably)
Menu: Breakfast specials served until 10.30 a.m. beans on toast, eggs on toast (scrambled or poached), bacon sandwich.

Lunch menu: sandwiches and toasted sandwiches with a variety of fillings, jacket potatoes with fillings, a choice of soup with roll, toasted teacakes, toasted muffin and lemon curd. Fairly traded coffee and decaffeinated coffee, tea and fruit tea, soft drinks, biscuits.

 Started in 1996. At present the church does not have its own building – worship is held in the local school. A shop unit became available and it was felt right to pursue a vision for a coffee shop / bookshop with a prayer room as a tangible expression of the church's presence on the estate.

Pleasant environment, good value for money ... people in the community more aware of our presence and involvement in community events ... Valuable source for people getting to know each other ... Links with local shops, schools, residential home.

See **Churches Working Together**

WEDNESBURY

WESLEY CENTRE

Wednesbury Central Methodist Church
Spring Head
Wednesbury
WS10 95X

Open: Monday to Saturday 10 a.m. – 12.30 p.m.
Staff: 25 volunteers.
Menu: Tea, coffee, soft drinks, biscuits.

Started in 1986 as a form of social outreach.

The drop-in facility was originally supported by Social Services with counselling and medical back up. They have withdrawn but a partnership with the Local Authority still exists in a day-care facility operated by the church ... It has become a form of mutual support / companionship for the elderly and a place where residents from a local centre for people with learning difficulties can meet with other people ... Some whose first contact was the Wesley Centre have become involved in the church.

John Wesley visited Wednesbury many times and in November 1745 met John Frederick Lampe, a musician and composer. 'I spent an hour with Mr

Lampe who had been a Deist for many years, till it pleased God to bring him to a better mind.' (*Journal*, 29th November 1745). John Wesley's favourite tune composed by J. S. Lampe was called 'Wednesbury'.

See **What's in a Name?**

WESTCLIFFE-ON-SEA

Trinity Methodist Church
515 London Road
Westcliffe-on-Sea
Essex S50 9LJ

TRINITY METHODIST CHURCH SHOP

Open: Monday to Saturday 10 a.m. – 4 p.m.
Staff: 10 volunteers
Menu: Tea, coffee, soft drinks, sandwiches, toasted sandwiches, jacket potatoes, egg, cheese, beans on toast, curries, crumpets, scones, bread puddings, cakes, salads, trifles, jelly, ice cream, rice pudding.

Started in 1996 to raise money for the church refurbishment.
Clean, warm, friendly, cheap and it's somewhere people can come for a chat ... Operates in conjunction with our charity shop.

WHITEHAVEN

The Parish of Whitehaven
St Nicholas Church Centre
Lowther Street
Whitehaven, Cumbria
www.victoria116.freeserve.co.uk

ST NICHOLAS CENTRE

Open: Monday to Saturday 10 a.m. – 4 p.m.
Staff: 70 volunteers serving about 1,300 people a week
Menu: Tea, coffee, hot chocolate, milk, Tip Top, minerals, squash, fresh orange, apple juice, Flintstones. Sandwiches and toasties with a variety of fillings, soup, bread, toast, biscuit, cakes (endless variety!)

Started in 1985 to use the remains of a church which was burned down in 1971.

Friendly, good food, inexpensive ... Became a vital part of the community ... The jewel in Whitehaven's crown.

Various charities and churches staff the café on Saturdays, e.g. Age Concern, Sea Cadets, Air Cadets, Senior Schools Link with (Rungwe) Tanzania, Scouts, Male Voice Choir, Diabetic Association. Worship in the Centre on Thursday at 10.30 a.m. and Sunday at 3 p.m.

See **Change and Renewal** and **Behind the Scenes**

WIGAN METHODIST MISSION   46 Market Street
                                                      Wigan
QUEEN'S HALL COFFEE BAR   WN1 1HX

Open: Monday to Saturday 10 a.m. - 1 p.m.
Staff: 40 volunteers
Menu: Soup and roll, toasted teacakes, toast, scones, fruit pie, tea, coffee, milk, orange cordial.

Started in the 1970s in the Old Queen's Hall (a typical city centre mission) and given a shop-front location in the new premises near the bus station. Between 350 and 400 people a week visit the café.

A local meeting point. Shoppers' refreshment. Lonely people depend on it ... The volunteers enjoy the fellowship and listening to and sometimes praying with troubled people.

WILLENHALL   Portobello Methodist Church
                                                  New Street
                                         Portobello, Willenhall
COMMUNITY CARE DROP-IN   Staffs WV13

Open: Wednesday 10 a.m. - 4 p.m.
Staff: 15 volunteers
Menu: Tea, coffee, squash, cake, toast. Cooked meals e.g. roasts, chops, shepherd's pie.

Started in 1990 to give a service to the community and most people come for the company.

Before the Drop-In opened people in the community were very much against the church but now there is a much warmer response to it ... At one time the community was split into two. The Drop-In has to some extent brought these groups together.

WIMBLEDON

Raynes Park Methodist Church
195–205 Worple Road
London

LANTERN COFFEE SHOP

SW20 8NU

Open: Monday to Friday 10 a.m. – 2 p.m.
Staff: 1 part time co-ordinator and 40 volunteers
Menu: Drinks, snacks, soup, sandwiches.

Started in 1996 as part of the rebirth of this church to provide an informal meeting place and listening ear service in the town centre.
A sense of being involved in the community. Working together with other churches and the Volunteer Bureau ... Helping others – some volunteers have gone on to employment ... Some people have been brought into the worshiping life of the church through being volunteers or customers.

See **Change and Renewal**

WIMBLEDON

St Luke's Church
Wimbledon Park
London

OPEN DOOR

Open: Wednesday morning
Staff: 12 volunteers
Menu: Coffee, tea, cakes, biscuits.

Started in 1985 as a focus socially for elderly members. It's always there on Wednesdays for the 15–20 who drop in on their way to the shops. As a result of Open Door the church is now open daily.

WINCHESTER
(Methodist and United Reformed)

The United Church
Jewry Street
Winchester

COFFEE BAR

Open: Monday to Friday 10 a.m. - 2 p.m.
Saturday 10 a.m. - 12 noon
Staff: 60-80 volunteers
Menu: Tea, coffee (filter, instant, decaffeinated), squash, apple juice, orange juice, soup, hot chocolate, Horlicks, rolls, cheese, butter, sandwiches, scones and butter, toast, toasted buns, biscuits.

Started in 1991 when Methodist and United Reformed Churches came together to form a united church in the refurbished ex-URC premises. One of the main priorities in the brief given to the architect was to make the church, by means of a coffee bar, more accessible to everyone and to serve the community.

Friendly staff - Somewhere for mums to bring children - No use of mobile phones! ... The volunteers have been enriched by meeting people they would not otherwise have known ... It is great to see people meeting friends and to hear the laughter but we also serve people who are sad and just want a quiet place to sit.
(Not able to cope with coach parties arriving unannounced!)

WISHAW

Old Parish Church
110 Main Street
Wishaw, Scotland
ML2 7NP

Open: Monday, Wednesday, Friday, Saturday 10 a.m. - 1 p.m.
Staff: 40 volunteers serving between 600 and 800 each week.
Most of the volunteers hold the 'Royal Environmental Institute of Scotland Food Hygiene Certificate'
Menu: Tea, coffee, juice, home baking - rolls and sausage rolls and gammon. Crisps, biscuits etc.

Started in 1962.

To help fund our mission and aid allocation ... The result has been that five groups of 16+ and five groups of adults have been sponsored on trips to Sinai, Israel and Oberammergau 2000. Monitoring and door opening devices have been placed in individual homes. Two motorised wheelchairs donated to a hospice and one to an individual ... A great meeting place for the elderly and young mothers with prams ... Cheap, high standards, wheelchair access, baby changing facilities and friendly staff.

WOKING

THE BEACON

Christ Church
Town Square
Woking, Surrey
GU21 1YG

Open: Monday to Friday 10 a.m. - 2 p.m.
Saturday 10.30 a.m. - 1.30 p.m.
Staff: 7 part time and 36 volunteers
Menu: Sandwiches, jacket potatoes, quiche, soup, hot dish, salads, cakes, ice cream, biscuits, hot and cold drinks.

Started in 1991 as part of a vision for the church to reach the wider community. Seats 66 and also provides 3 high chairs and a Lego table. Between 180 and 200 people a day enjoy a high standard of food served by pleasant staff at average prices. 'It's good value,' say the customers who keep returning, especially young mums and the over fifties. The town centre site provides good access for the disabled. There is good fellowship between the regular staff and volunteers who have 'fun at work' and begin each day with a prayer time. Profits from the café have helped to finance youth projects and the appointment of a counsellor.

WORTHING

WELCOME IN

The Salvation Army
Crescent Road
Worthing, West Sussex
BN11 1RL

Open: Monday to Friday 10 a.m. - 4 p.m.
Staff: 4 full time and 12 volunteers

Menu: Hot and cold drinks (tea, coffee, chocolate, soft drinks), breakfasts, lunches, snacks including cakes, sausage rolls, pies, quiches, salads, baked potatoes, sandwiches, various toasts with fillings, crisps, chocolate.

Started in 1992 as a service to the local community. All age groups come, some needy – some quite affluent. 100–150 people a day.

Much effort is taken to make customers feel happy and that it is a pleasure to serve them ... Lonely people attend and make friends here ... There is always a happy buzz about the place ... Plenty of Christian literature around ... Always someone available if spiritual counselling is needed ... The Welcome In is part of a larger community programme in which the Salvation Army touches lives practically and spiritually.

YORK   St Michaels Church
                                                    Spurriergate
THE SPURRIERGATE CENTRE   YO1 9QR
                                      www.thespurriergatecentre.com

Open: Monday to Friday 10 a.m. - 4.30 p.m.
        Saturday 8.30 a.m. - 5 p.m.
Staff: 37 a mixture of full time and volunteers serving 3,000 people per week
Menu: Daily specials – dish of the day; wholesome cheesy quiche, herby cheese and potato square (all with fresh salad or vegetables); Yorkshires with meat and seasonal vegetables and gravy (or vegetables only); freshly made sandwiches and jacket potatoes with exciting fillings; soup and roll, sausage rolls. Desserts. Coffee, tea etc. fairly traded.

Started in 1989 to make good use of a redundant church building.
Child friendly, good access, great service, strong local centre for ecumenical witness.

See **Change and Renewal**

St Sampson's Church
Church Street
York
YO1 8BE

ST SAMPSON'S
A Day Centre for the Over Sixties

Open: Tuesday to Saturday 10 a.m. - 4 p.m.
Staff: 1 full time, 5 part time and 80 volunteers
Menu: Tea, coffee, fruit juices. Ham, egg, tuna, corned beef and other assorted sandwiches. Pie and peas, soup, salads, scones, cakes and toasted teacakes.

Started in 1974 in a redundant church to provide a facility for pensioners (warmth, friendship, companionship and value for money). 1,000 people per week visit the centre.

See **Change and Renewal**

Where they are ...

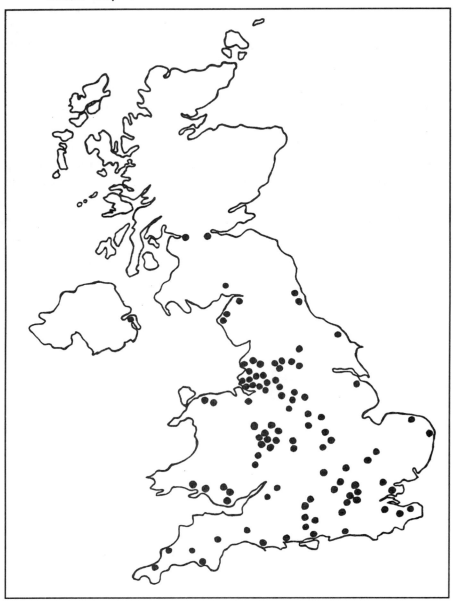

... now find them.

What's in a Name?

Some cafés seem comfortable enough adopting the name of the church, whilst others have thought the matter through very carefully as parents do when choosing a name for their new baby. At Kimberley Baptist Church, for instance, they considered 'Loaves and Fishes', 'Bread of Life', 'Living Waters' before deciding on **Different Aspects**. The café expresses one aspect of Christian outreach into the community, but in the same building worship, teaching, fellowship groups, the bookstore and work among children and young people are all meeting particular needs both physically and spiritually in an atmosphere of love, warmth, prayer and encouragement. **The Welcome Bap** at Chard brings together a familiar word with one that is intriguing. The 'bap' originates from a shortened form of 'Baptist' and because at one time the café's speciality was a bread bap with a choice of fillings.

When the café on the Fairfield Estate in Buxton was opened, and named **The Pepperpot**, for some reason the choice surprised me until I realised that it was conveying the same message as **Salt Cellar**, a café I had visited in Oldham. Salt and pepper add flavour, and a priority of any church café must be to add value to life in the community. Some names will be open to more than one interpretation.

In this chapter we focus on four biblical names, five associated with people, and three related to particular places.

THE SYCAMORE TREE

Luke 19.1-10

The Sycamore Tree at **Larkfield** in Kent was a response to the New Start Initiative for the Millennium. The ground floor of the Church Centre was completely refurbished and opened as a coffee shop to provide a meeting place for the local community on weekday mornings. It is child friendly, reasonably priced, and is creating a community resource for networking. But why the Sycamore Tree?

Trees have long been famous as 'trysting' or meeting places. There is the old Major Oak in Sherwood Forest, Nottingham, where Robin Hood and his Merrie Men are said to have gathered. The great sycamore tree in Tolpuddle, Dorset, near the Methodist Chapel, is where the famous Tolpuddle Martyrs met to discuss their desires to protect the working people, and planted the seeds from which the Trade Union movement was to grow.

In the Bible there is a story in the New Testament of how Jesus met Zacchaeus, a tax collector. Zacchaeus was very short and climbed up into a nearby sycamore tree to see Jesus better. Jesus knew he was there and called him down saying he wanted to eat and drink with him and share his company.

So the Sycamore Tree is a place to meet old friends, make new ones, to chat and to share food and drink. Perhaps it's also worth noting part of verse 3 in St Luke chapter 19: 'He could not see him for the crowd.' Churches that are crowded are seemingly models of success, but individuals can be lost in a crowd. Smaller groups must be created for real meeting between people to take place. This is more likely to happen round a café table than sitting in rows of pews or chairs where only the backs of heads are visible.

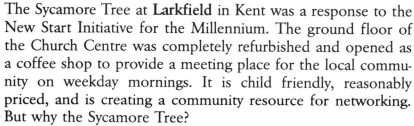

Cornerstone

Ephesians 2.20 and 1 Peter 2, 4 & 5

A careful study of the New Testament reveals fifty-five names or titles given to Jesus. Some are well known, such as Son of God, Son of Man, Saviour, Shepherd, Christ, Lord. Others are less conspicuous but important, such as Alpha and Omega, Bridegroom, Word, the Last Adam, the Amen and the Stone. In Ephesians 2.20 St Paul addresses those new first-century Christians: 'You are built on the foundation of the apostles and prophets, with Christ Jesus himself as the cornerstone.' Peter in his first letter speaks of Jesus as 'a choice cornerstone of great worth'. He invites the young in the faith, 'newborn infants craving for pure milk to come to him, our living stone ... come and let yourselves be built, as living stones, into a spiritual temple.'

Two hymns from the sixth or seventh centuries take up this powerful image:

> Christ is made the sure foundation,
> Christ the head and cornerstone.
>
> Christ is our cornerstone,
> On Him alone we build.

So at **Ashbourne, Chesterfield** and **Cirencester** the name outside is loaded with meaning and directly related to a New Testament image of Jesus and to those who would be followers of him.

One of the volunteers at Chesterfield Methodist Cornerstone told me that whilst the café / bookshop is at the corner of the building, that fact alone was not responsible for the choice of name. 'At the time of the redevelopment in 1985, the small committee charged with the setting up of the shop quickly came up with the name. We all saw Christ as the cornerstone of everything that we hoped to achieve in the considerable redevelopment of the premises. There was much more to it than bricks and mortar! We often sang "God is working His purpose out ...", which seemed so appropriate with the emphasis on the opening lines of the last verse: "All we can do is nothing worth, unless God blesses the deed." '

Manna

Exodus 16: 14, 15

> And when the dew that lay was gone up, behold, upon the face of the wilderness there lay a small round thing, as small as the hoar frost on the ground. And when the children of Israel saw it, they said one to another, it is MANNA: for they wist not what it was. And Moses said unto them, This is the bread which the Lord hath given you to eat.

The verses quoted are from the Authorised Version of the Bible. Other translations put part of verse 15 in the form of a question:

> When the Israelites saw it, they said to one another, 'What is it?'

That's what Manna means: 'What is it?' On discovering this mysterious substance to be edible, Moses gives instructions: 'Gather as much of it as each of you needs, an omer* to a person ... Let no one leave any of it over until morning ... On the sixth day gather double to cover the Sabbath.' St John's Gospel, chapter 6, relates this to Jesus as bread of life and in two communion hymns manna is referred to as 'sent from heaven' and 'life imparting'. This link between food for the journey supplied in the wilderness and feeding on Christ in the Eucharist makes an important connecting link between Old and New Testaments.

Liskeard Manna was started to be a bridge between the street and the church and a sales outlet for Christian books, greetings cards and Traidcraft items. It is open every weekday morning serving home-made cakes, biscuits, coffee, tea, canned and bottled fruit drinks. 300 people per week come through the doors, with 50 volunteers staffing the enterprise. Among the volunteers it has given a sense of fulfilment as sharers in the mission of the Servant Church. Some who live alone come several times a week and it has become known as a supportive calling place for promoting community concerns. Profits are allocated to local and national good causes.

---

* An omer is a Hebrew dry measure of just over two-and-a-quarter litres.

Manna links Liskeard with **Notting Hill** where **Manna Café** is part of the ministry and outreach of the Parish of St John and St Peter. Manna is located in a secluded and quiet courtyard on the Portobello Road, so it is full of tourists when the market is on and the rest of the time it serves the local community. The site was built in 1862 as a church school for deprived children, and continued as such until the 1920s. Thereafter it was used as a fine art printworks. The café is now situated where the presses used to be. These reproduced the works of contemporary artists, including David Hockney and Henry Moore. In 1991 the building reverted to the parish and now is a base for community activities, e.g. nursery school, artists' studios, arts and drama classes, various support groups, community meetings and Manna Café.

Manna seeks to provide delicious, innovative, good value food with a weekly changing seasonal menu. As much produce as possible is either bought from organisations that encourage fair trade, or is sourced from local suppliers.

Our aim is that Manna will provide a place where people can drink, eat, talk and rest at leisure, in a friendly and relaxed atmosphere.

Our wish is that you should leave Manna feeling refreshed.
We are here to offer friendship, or help in any way.
You only have to let us know.

The Saints

Romans 1.7; Philippians 1.1
Ephesians 1.1; Colossians 1.2

The spire at **Chesterfield** Parish Church is a wonderful eye-catcher and a tourist attraction. 'It stands most curiously awry,' wrote an eighteenth-century traveller. The spire is constructed of Spanish chestnut covered in thirty-two tons of lead, placed in a herring-bone design. Legend has it that balks of timber eighty feet long were towed from Spain behind ships, then carried overland to Chesterfield. The twist in the spire was caused by the heat of the sun drawing the moisture content from the timber, which was not fully seasoned at the time.

The coffee shop is across the road in the Saints Parish Centre. Both the attractive menus and serviettes feature the spire, but the name is linked to the magnificent fourteenth-century church below the spire, called St Mary and All Saints or Our Lady and All Saints, and prior to the Reformation simply All Saints.

In each of the biblical references provided, St Paul is greeting the saints. Lest we get carried away with the idea that they were among the spiritual elite, the word in New Testament Greek refers to all God's dedicated people. A church called *All* Saints retains this emphasis as do modern translations of the New Testament, e.g. 'Paul and Timothy, servants of Christ Jesus to *all the saints* in Christ Jesus which are at Philippi' (Authorised Version). 'From Paul and Timothy, servants of Christ Jesus, to *all God's people* at Philippi who are incorporate in Christ Jesus' (Revised English Bible).

Certainly this prayer may apply to the two dozen volunteers who serve 100 people a day:

> Lord of all pots and pans and things ...
> make me a saint by getting meals and
> washing up the plates.

Fuller

Fuller

COFFEE HOUSE

When a scheme for redeveloping **Kettering** town centre included the exchange of some land owned by Fuller Baptist Church on Gold Street for new premises in Newlands Shopping Centre, it was decided to open a Coffee House to extend the mission of the church. The church is named after its famous minister, Andrew Fuller, who was also a founder member and the first General Secretary of the Baptist Missionary Society which was formed in Kettering in 1792.

Andrew Fuller was born in Wicken, Cambridgeshire, in 1754 and was minister at Soham 1775–1782. Then he moved to Kettering where he served as minister until his death in May 1815.

Fuller's commitment to, and enthusiasm for, the BMS was founded on his theology. He took the lead in the fight against hyper-Calvinism. His views were expressed in his book, *The Gospel Worthy of All Acceptation*, which was published in 1785. Fuller found himself continually facing criticism but 'Fullerism', as it became known, gained ground and the hold of hyper-Calvinism on Baptist ministers was weakened.

For over twenty years the home organisation of the BMS depended on Andrew Fuller. He had no office and the Society was only one of many demands on his time. He was minister of a local church, theologian and author. It is estimated that he spent about three months of every year travelling and preaching on behalf of the Society.

His desk was in the sitting-room, and he worked with his family around him. Under such circumstances he penned all his letters to the missionaries, copied in his own hand and circulated the important part of their replies and generally conducted all the work of the Committee.

In this one man lay the embryo for future growth. A note on his death reads, 'The loss which the Society has sustained by the death of our indefatigable secretary is such as the exertions of no individual can repair.' That was prophetic, for at the next Annual Meeting it was agreed, 'that the Revd James Hinton of Oxford be requested to act as joint secretary with Dr Ryland for the ensuing year and that they be empowered to procure what assistance in office they may need, at the expense of the Society.'

The expense of the Society to that point had been a payment to Fuller to enable him to appoint an assistant minister for the church.

The Unfinished Story, The Baptist Missionary Society

The church has a Heritage Room containing memorabilia of the past. 'Whilst we are proud of our history,' says the welcome leaflet, 'we are also aware that we ourselves are called to be "history-makers" by using every opportunity for sharing the Good News of Jesus Christ and expressing the love of God. A fine example of this is our modern Coffee House, in Newland Street, where you can find friendship and help as well as friendly and efficient service.'

A few full-time or part-time staff, plus forty volunteers including a team of young people on Saturdays, serve between 200 and 300 people per day. Queues often form outside the doors on the busy Newlands Street ten minutes before opening time. Since it was opened in December 1990 it has become a landmark in the area. For many people it is a place to take a break during a shopping trip, somewhere to grab a quick snack or meet friends and family. For others it is where they will find a warm smile and someone to talk to.

As part of the outreach a Befriending Service was started to give customers a more intimate point of contact. Information about this is prominently displayed.

On each table is a box containing literature. It is a mixture of information about the church, what it means to be a Christian, and small booklets looking at specific aspects of life. How this literature is used, or may make a difference in someone's life, nobody knows. What the staff at Fuller do know is that the boxes continually need to be refilled!

Befriending Service

We try to create a friendly atmosphere in our Coffee House where you may relax with your refreshments. In addition if you are troubled by a personal problem our Befriending Service is here to help you.

We now have a Befriending Room where you may talk in private with a Befriender who will listen, understand and support. See our pink leaflet or have a quiet word with any member of staff.

Wesley

There are eight Wesley Cafés listed in the Directory (maybe the ecclesiastical equivalent of Tetleys!). They're all Methodist, of course, and a link with the Wesley brothers, John and Charles, and their part in the rise of Methodism in the eighteenth century. It should be noted, however, that this remarkable family was bound up with English religious, musical and cultural life for over two hundred years. John Wesley, a Dorset Rector and grandfather of his more famous namesake, dissented from the Church of England in 1662 along with hundreds of clergy who were unable to accept Charles the Second's Act of Uniformity. Some of John's children remained life-long nonconformists, but one son, Samuel, made his peace with the established Church and became a country parson in Lincolnshire. He was a faithful parish priest and prolific writer. Nineteen children were born to Samuel and his wife Susannah at Epworth Rectory. Ten children survived infancy including John and Charles. If John's preaching was at the heart of the Evangelical Revival, it was Charles who made it possible for new converts to sing their faith. 'And can it be ...', 'O for a thousand tongues to sing ...', 'O thou who camest from above ...' are but three examples of the six thousand or more hymns written by Charles Wesley. One of his sons, Samuel, became a composer and his grandson, Samuel Sebastian, was organist of Hereford Cathedral (1832-5), of Exeter Cathedral (1836-42), of Winchester Cathedral (1849-65) and of Gloucester Cathedral

(1865-76). 'In Quires and places where they sing,' (to quote the Book of Common Prayer) the name of S.S. Wesley is to be found as the composer of Anthems such as 'Lead me, Lord' and 'Blessed be the God and Father'.

It's quite probable, however, that cafés baptised into the

name of Wesley may have had John in mind rather than the whole family. As he covered the country on horseback, he kept a careful record of his travels in shorthand, later to be deciphered by Nehemiah Curnock and published as a *Journal* in several volumes. He was able to ride and read – leaving his horse with a loose rein to find its own way along the rough tracks.

Occasionally in the *Journal* two words appear: 'I dined.' Little seems to be known about John Wesley's eating preferences, but we do know that Josiah Wedgwood made him a beautiful teapot with the words of a Grace on it:

> Be present at our Table Lord
> Be here and everywhere ador'd
> These creatures bless & grant that we
> May feast in Paradise with thee.

In July 1746, however, the *Journal* records Wesley's decision to give up tea drinking and among his letters is one to a friend, written from Newington in 1748, extolling the health and financial benefits he has accrued from two years without tea.

John Wesley had something to record in his *Journal* about most places that have Wesley Cafés today. For instance, there are two contrasting entries, separated by thirty years, with reference to his visits to **Nottingham**.

> Friday, 21st March 1746 I came to Nottingham. I had long doubted what it was which hindered the work of God here. But upon inquiry the case was plain. So many of the society were either triflers or disorderly walkers, that the blessing of God could not rest, upon them; so I made short work, cutting off all such at a stroke, and leaving only that little handful who (as far as could be judged) were really in earnest to save their souls.

> Wednesday, 18th July 1777 I preached at Nottingham, to a serious, loving congregation. There is something in the people of this town, which I cannot but much approve of; although most of our

society are of the lower class, chiefly employed in the stocking manufacture, yet there is generally an uncommon gentleness and sweetness in their temper, and something of elegance in their behaviour, which, when added to solid, vital religion, make them an ornament to their profession.

 At the heart of London, opposite Westminster Abbey and the Houses of Parliament, is a Wesley Café at Methodist Central Hall, **Westminster**. The Central Hall is sometimes seen on television as the venue for important public meetings. In that capacity the Hall has welcomed many great gatherings including the Inaugural Meeting of The United Nations. The basement, used in war time as an air-raid shelter, is now Wesley's Café. This modern cafeteria with seating for 200 is open each day, including Sunday, for breakfast, lunch and afternoon tea. This is part of the church's daily ministry, 'Where cross the crowded ways of life'.

The most recent café to be named Wesley's is at **Harpenden** where Methodism has strong roots going back to 1790. The church on the High Street was built in 1930 and since the mid-70s an upstairs coffee lounge has been a popular meeting place in the town. In recent years there has been a desire to build on that success and make the facility more accessible by moving it to the ground floor with direct access from the glass-fronted High Street foyer and the car park at the rear of the church.

After years of consideration as part of the church's Opening Doors Challenge and months of planning, building and fund-raising, it all came together for the dedication and opening in February 2002. '... And it looks great! The walls are pale yellow, and the chairs are blond bentwood with blue upholstery. A "beaten bronze" glaze over volcanic red enlivens the front of the servery. There are settees, easy chairs and bar stools ...' During the course of the scheme, church members have been kept fully informed and encouraged to be involved in the venture. This has attracted voluntary labour, direct giving, fund-raising and participation in detailed planning. In order to furnish the new café, pledges were invited from the congregation to cover the cost of various items, e.g. chairs, tables, high chairs, trays, freezer, toaster, crockery, cutlery, curtains, display boards and pictures.

A competition was organised to name the café and Wesley's was chosen. A logo was designed and a mission statement prepared:

> *As an integral part of the church's life and witness, we aim to demonstrate God's love for people of all ages, and to be a link between community and church, through serving a range of quality refreshments at affordable prices in a warm, welcoming, caring and comfortable environment.*

The Methodist emphasis on 'Fellowship' fostered by the Wesley-style class meeting is a link with the café culture of our time. The various projects allied to cafés featured in this book are directly related to the Wesley search for wholeness of body, mind and spirit. For John Wesley and the early Methodists the Christian Faith was worked out in down-to-earth, practical ways (e.g. promoting education, writing helpful books and tracts for the times, opening dispensaries and orphanages, visiting prisons and mines). A week before his death in 1791, Wesley wrote to the young William Wilberforce encouraging him in his fight against the 'execrable villainy' of slavery.

Another connecting link between Wesley and cafés is the output of ceramics following his death. On souvenir cups, saucers, mugs, plates and dishes his last words appeared: 'The best of all is, God is with us.'

Bunyan

Bunyan Meeting Free Church in **Bedford** was formed in 1650 by a group of twelve with John Gifford as its first minister. John Bunyan, converted under Gifford's ministry, was imprisoned at this time for preaching without a licence. Shortly before his release he was called to be the minister, remaining in office until his death in 1688. John Bunyan and others purchased a barn and part of an orchard on Mill Street in 1672. The first purpose-built church was erected in 1707. This was demolished and replaced by the present building in 1850. Further buildings were added in 1868 and 1892. The church was renovated and refurbished in 1974. Its architectural features have been preserved with imaginative use of glass panels, simple decor, effective lighting and comfortable chairs making it functional, but retaining its worshipful atmosphere.

The café is situated in the church foyer and was opened in 1988 to provide refreshments for visitors who came to the church and museum during a

The John Bunyan Museum in its new building, opened in 1998, tells the story of this renowned author, born in humble circumstances in the parish of Elstow, near Bedford, in 1628. See how the laws in force in 17th-century England put Bunyan in prison for expressing his religious beliefs.

Follow in his footsteps through Bedford's cobbled streets, stand in a pulpit where he preached and visit him in his prison cell.

countrywide festival of commemoration for the tercentenary of John Bunyan's death. Since then it has welcomed thousands of people whose first step over the threshold of this historic church is greeted by the cosiness of the café. The name **Open Doors** is a good link with Bunyan whose writings from prison remind us that his faith

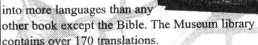

John Bunyan portrayed characters and events in such a way that his writing went on to become world famous. *The Pilgrim's Progress*, published in 1678, has been translated into more languages than any other book except the Bible. The Museum library contains over 170 translations.

enabled him to transcend stone walls and iron bars to be gloriously free within. His emphasis was on the Christian life as a pilgrimage, a movement through many open doors.

Terry Waite, the mediator held hostage for over five years in Beirut, received a postcard showing this window of John Bunyan writing the *Pilgrim's Progress* in prison. Upon his release he spoke highly of the way the message gave him hope and uplifted his spirits during his solitary confinement in Beirut.

Dale

The entrance, the threshold, of any building is of immense importance in determining our first impression of the household or organisation we are visiting. It is a place where we allow observation of minute detail to assume great significance as we attempt – within the space of perhaps only a few seconds – to get the feel of what we are letting ourselves in for. It is also a place of decision, of momentary hesitation, in the split second before the door opens and a new encounter is set in motion.

– RICHARD GILES, *Re-Pitching the Tent: re-ordering the church building for worship and mission in the new millennium*
Canterbury Press, 1996

The entrance to Carrs Lane United Reformed Church in **Birmingham** city centre is both spacious and welcoming. In this area is a statue of Robert William Dale, minister of the church from 1859 to 1895. Founded as a Congregational church in 1748, it is now in its fourth building which was completed in 1970. The Carrs Lane Church Centre is the home of many caring organisations and of a bookshop. Downstairs from the main church complex, but accessible by a separate entrance, is Dale Pantry Cafeteria.

The cafeteria consists of a 60-seater restaurant with the capacity to seat a further 30 customers in a private dining area. It is an extremely flexible establishment that can cater for shoppers in the main cafeteria and can also provide a luncheon club facility in the private dining area. It also offers a sandwich service to local offices and beverage and buffets to private meetings and functions within the church centre.

Dale Pantry Cafeteria aims to offer a place where all members of the community can meet and eat during the day, in an atmosphere of friendship and calm, a welcome break from the hustle and bustle of city life.

During his long ministry, Dr Dale entered into the civic life of Birmingham. He was especially interested in education and in dealing with the fundamental causes of poverty and crime. His political activity was an important part of his work, but he never introduced party politics into the pulpit. The Carrs Lane congregation was inspired to be involved in the world as Christian citizens and to be active in voluntary service.

The Dale ethos lives on and expresses itself in today's Carrs Lane and the way the church seeks to respond to the needs of the people of Birmingham.

Tookey

When, in 1643, Job Tookey was appointed by Oliver Cromwell as Lecturer or Preacher in **St Ives** he could not possibly have foreseen that 350 years later his name would be given to a coffee shop! According to the *Oxford Dictionary of the Christian Church*, lecturers in the sixteenth and seventeenth centuries were unordained ministers appointed by Parliament to particular parishes and charged with lecturing in church on the Christian faith. The system, which was especially popular with the Puritans, was bitterly resisted by most of the clergy. The lecturer was supported voluntarily by the parishioners on whose recommendation he was usually appointed. *The Journals of Parliament* from 1641 to 1643 mention the appointment of some 190 lecturers.

The Free Church in St Ives can trace its origins to Cromwell who lived in the town. His statue stands outside the building in Market Hill which was opened in 1864 and extensively re-ordered in 1979-80. The flexible premises facilitate a wide range of social, cultural and welfare activities as the church seeks to reach out into the community. The ground floor includes a spacious entrance, a Fair Trade Shop, 'Just Sharing', and leads into Tookeys. So there's more to St Ives than the well-known rhyme:

> As I was going to St Ives
> I met a man with seven wives.
> Each wife had seven sacks,
> Each sack had seven cats,
> Each cat had seven kits.
> Kits, cats, sacks and wives,
> How many were going to St Ives?

And this one is not in Cornwall!

The Discovery Centre

From **Plymouth** many have set out on voyages of discovery. Little wonder then that a church situated in Drake Circus should name its café and bookshop The Discovery Centre. Plymouth Central Hall is a vibrant city centre Methodist Mission. In this church over the years thousands of people have taken the long journey inwards to discover themselves and their relationship with God. This has often resulted in a journey outwards to serve God in the world and to discover him there.

The Discovery Centre, which opened in November 1997, runs down one side of Central Hall, facing one of the main shopping streets in Plymouth. There is a 90-seat café with additional seating in good weather on a terrace outside. At the front of the centre is a shop selling an excellent range of Christian books and CDs, fairly traded products from Traidcraft and Tearcraft and other goods from local sources. At the other end of the café is a beautifully appointed prayer chapel, available for private prayer and used for worship during the week.

The aim of the café is to provide good, freshly cooked food in a relaxed and friendly atmosphere. There is easy access for prams and wheelchairs, baby feeding facilities, high chairs and a fenced play area for children. On the café tables, display boards and in the bookshop there is plenty of information about the Christian faith and the activities of the church. There is always someone on hand to talk to or to pray with those who may express a need.

> The gospel has long been shared over a meal. Perhaps Matthew was the first, with the party he threw after Jesus had called him from his provincial tax office. Many of his tax-collector friends were there and we can imagine him introducing them to Jesus. A meal is common ground, something nearly all of us are able to enjoy. Matthew's approach to evangelism lies behind the Discovery Centre – the café is our opportunity to introduce Jesus.

117

The Stable

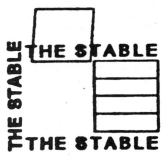

When the Methodist and United Reformed Churches in **Newmarket** joined together in 1994, the United Reformed premises on the High Street opposite Boots were converted into a meeting place for the local community. This initiative is known as The Stable. It offers an excellent modern environment with ease of access for disabled people, including a lift to the first floor coffee bar. There is a voucher scheme offering homeless people food and refreshment. The Stable provides a venue for over twenty organisations in the town.

The attractive menu advertises a range of home-cooked food and over 500 people per week are well pleased with it. Six staff are employed on a part-time basis and voluntary helpers work alongside them in a variety of practical ways. In addition a facility for teenagers to socialise in the non-alcoholic bar and games room, within a safe environment, operates on a Friday evening.

OPEN
7.00 pm – 10 pm

Every FRIDAY

Q. So what is the Teens Bar?

A. The Teens Bar is a non-alcoholic drop-in bar for young people between the ages of 13 and 17 years, this means they can come and go as they wish. It is not a youth club and no subscription for membership is charged.

Q. Are there any activities?

A. The Games Room offers 2 pool tables, table tennis and a playstation. The Hall is large enough for a supervised game of football (a foam football supplied by The Stable is only to be used.) The Coffee Bar offers a place to play board games or just sit and chat with friends.

Q. Does my child need any money?

A. Yes, a refundable deposit of £1 is required to use the foam football.

Q. Are refreshments available?

A. Yes, hot and cold drinks. Light snacks, crisps and chocolate bars (all at very reasonable prices). Delicious home-made cakes. A menu is on display in the Coffee Bar.

Q. What do young people get from the Teens Bar?

A. A safe, friendly and drug/alcohol-free environment, where they can meet friends, listen to music (they can bring CDs and tapes) or participate in the activities mentioned.

Racing at Newmarket provides an obvious link with The Stable and voyagers setting out from Plymouth with The Discovery. The connection between name and place is less obvious in the next illustration.

Pie in the Sky

Eastenders know that the United Reformed Church on Bruce Road, **Bromley-by-Bow** is not just the house of God, but provides a home for his people. It's a Worship Centre, but also a workshop within the community. With befitting irony the witness of this church is a powerful antidote to the criticism sometimes made of religion that it is nothing more than 'pie in the sky when you die', or what Karl Marx called 'the opium of the people'.

The purpose of the café is to be 'a beacon of high quality in a deprived area'. It provides a much-needed facility to serve the community and also training, employment and enterprise opportunities for local people. Pie in the Sky has recently moved into a purpose-built area within the New Church Complex. It is open twelve hours a day (8 a.m. – 8 p.m.). There are changing daytime and evening menus with the salad bar offering such delicacies as spicy peppers, mushrooms and onions; mixed seafood and avocado; apple-slaw and pine nuts with blue cheese dressing; artichoke, tomatoes, olives and basil; pasta and chicken medley. Main courses include: fish in curry and basil sauce with boiled potatoes and green beans; vegetable parcels with sauté potatoes, salad and spicy sauce; cheese, sweet pepper and tuna quiche, new potatoes and salad; meat loaf hunter style with roast potatoes and spinach; chicken escalope with chips and salad; pasta with ratatouille with cheese gratin. On Thursdays all day and on Friday evenings there is a Bangladeshi women's café called **Bandhobi**.

In addition the café bakes bread for services of Holy Communion and caters for after worship refreshment, social events, weddings and funerals. A pizza outlet is planned.

A Soperism recalled:

Donald Soper speaking in Hyde Park about the Kingdom of God as a present reality:

It's not pie in the sky when we die, but ham where we am.

Churches Working Together

Protestant cows,
 Won't milk on Sundays,
Puritan cows,
 Are dubious of mud;
Baptist cows,
 Get immersed in the waterways,
Anglican cows,
 Chew overmuch cud.
Romanist cows,
 Need plenary indulgence,
Methodist cows,
 Refuse barley and hops;
Adventist cows,
 Take a rest on Saturdays,
Orthodox cows,
 Are omphalloscopes.

Cows Unitarian,
 Boggle at the clover,
Genevan Calvinists
 Dislike lucerne;
Clairvoyant cows,
 Have a yield only medium,
Lutheran cows,
 Are faithful, but stern.
Salvationist cows,
Always trumpet like an elephant,
Brawly the cow Presbyterian,
 Hoots!
Strict and Particular,
 Low as they make 'em,
Quakers are silent,
 But friendly old brutes.

Thus, as the middlemen
 Come for the marketing,
Readily prepared
 With a number of churns,
Keeping the Catholic milk
 From the Protestant,
Lest in a quantity
 The aggregate turns.
All this variety
 Of vaccine devotion,
Poses a problem
 Experiment must solve:
For the triumph of reunion,
 How may the paragon
Lactiferous evolve?

How can we fashion
 The cow Ecumenical,
Worthy of leaping
 The moon at the full?
Surely by crossing
 The Protestant varieties
With an acceptable and strong
 Papal Bull.

121

I know not the source of those lines but acknowledge them with gratitude as a reflective starter to this section where the spotlight is put on churches working in partnership to create community cafés. How can we fashion the cow ecumenical? At the grass roots it often begins by working together in practical ways.

It's worth remembering that it is still less than a hundred years since some Christians began to take their disunity seriously. In 1910 at an International Missionary Conference held in Edinburgh it was recognised that strict adherence to denominationalism was a hindrance to Christian evangelism and, indeed, a scandal. From 1910 onwards the winds of change have been blowing. Local Councils of Churches were formed in Bolton and Manchester in 1917, addressing many joint concerns about social issues of the day. The Birmingham Conference in 1924 on Politics, Economics and Citizenship (COPEC) gave national encouragement to local initiatives. The British Council of Churches came into being in 1942 and following on from the Amsterdam Assembly of the World Council of Churches in 1948 the symbol of the church as a boat on the sea of the world with its mast in the shape of the cross became familiar.

By 1970 the number of local Councils of Churches had grown to 650. 'Not doing separately what we can better do together' became the slogan. The Week of Prayer for Christian Unity in January and Christian Aid Week in May strengthened relationships in many places. Whilst *top-down* schemes to bring churches together in one body have often floundered, *bottom-up* Local Ecumenical Partnerships or Covenants have flourished. What is now called the inter-church process encourages the releasing of energy through the sharing of resources. At best we now pursue the search for unity respecting the rich treasures of diversity. The Pilgrim Prayer of this inter-church process encapsulates for many of us the exciting stage we have reached as Christians journeying together, not as strangers but as pilgrims:

122

Lord God,
We thank you for calling us
Into the company of those who trust in Christ
And seek to obey his will.
You have made us strangers no longer
But pilgrims together
On the way to your kingdom.
Through Jesus Christ our Lord. Amen.

In a recent issue of *Together*, the news sheet for Churches Together in Nottinghamshire and Derbyshire, our Ecumenical Development Officer, the Revd Philip Webb wrote about his hobby, Meccano.

Occasionally I will branch out from my specialised subjects into something different - like a bridge, for instance. An ideal subject for Meccano, with all those girders and strips. I have sometimes thought that I should make up a medium sized model and take it around with me when I visit churches and Churches Together groups - an example of what each of us is about ... We often talk of our Lord as a carpenter (though the Greek word used might better be translated as 'general builder'). But we also call Him our Great High Priest. The Latin title for this is 'Pontifex Maximus' which means - the Great Bridge Builder!

The Bridge at Valley Church in **Andover** makes its intention clear on the menu:

The Bridge Coffee Shop is part of The Bridge, which has been set up by the Christian community in Andover to enable people and resources to meet. If we can be of any help to you or you would like to find out more about us, please ask a staff member.

Also on the menu is an interesting play on the word 'Bridge': Bridge Toasties; Bridge baked potatoes; Bridge salads; Bridge Bulge Builders. Young people are involved in this ministry so bridging the generation gap. Christians of different denominations share in serving 70 to 80 people a day who cross The Bridge into the café. So what a good name to put outside a Christian café and with which to baptise Manchester Cathedral's new visitors' centre.

We move on to look at ways in which bridges are built as churches work together exercising a ministry of hospitality.

The Rock

Christ Church on the **Woodloes Park Estate,** near **Warwick** is a Local Ecumenical Partnership: Anglicans, Baptists and Methodists working together. Their Mission Statement reads:

> *To be a worshipping, praying and witnessing presence on the Woodloes Park Estate, proclaiming the love of God shown to all in Jesus Christ. A community of disciples open to being nurtured and equipped by God through the leadership team and committed to being open, honest, sensitive, loving and welcoming to all people of any denomination or none.*

The Rock Coffee Shop was established to be a tangible expression of Christ's presence on the estate. It provides a meeting place for people of all ages and all needs. It has become a good place to make friends, have a chat and laugh, and to share problems. There are special days to support charities such as Comic Relief. Fairtrade Week is celebrated, Fairtrade goods sold, and Fairtrade tea and coffee served.

Once a term the Beginners Class from a nearby school comes for two sessions into the café. The children sit around the tables, place their own orders and observe the way in which waitress service operates.

A variety of Christian literature, message cards and videos are well displayed. Useful information (a mini Citizens Advice Bureau) is kept in an up-to-date file. The coffee shop opens up into an attractive worship area used for Sunday and mid-week worship.

The Crossroads Centre

Crossroads Centre

Fifteen years ago the six churches in **Great Crosby** formed an alliance to benefit the whole community. This bond united Roman Catholic, Anglican and Methodist Churches. The Crossroads Centre was established as a charitable trust and has become a focal point of visible ecumenism in the area. By working together the churches have made a significant contribution to community life through Crossroads' ministry. The café and drop-in centre is a well-known meeting place for people of all ages with its friendly atmosphere and reasonably priced refreshments.

Now the project itself is at the crossroads and moving to new premises later in the year. One thing is sure: the ministry will continue and develop.

Doves Coffee Lounge

'Fran's Food' is a column in the *Cumberland News and Star*. In July 2001 readers were asked to nominate 'the best Café in Cumbria'.

> Cavalcade of the Cuppas – You name names in our search for the café that is the cream of Cumbria.

At the end of the competition the *News and Star* headline proclaimed:

Doves is high flier in battle of caffs

Our search for the cream of Cumbrian cafés has come up with a clear winner. Doves coffee lounge on Chapel Street, Carlisle, came up trumps for its combination of delicious, nutritious food with excellent value for money and a relaxed atmosphere. There were many strong entries to the competition and we had difficulty judging which was the best. But in the end Doves, nominated by Rosemary Armstrong of Cargo, scored best across the board for quality and quantity of food, price and friendly service. The café is run by volunteers from Carlisle's twelve churches and a percentage of all the profits goes to the charity Christian Aid. Miss Armstrong said: 'There is a beautiful atmosphere in the café and all the volunteers are there because they want to be. There is always someone that can listen sympathetically and perhaps point you in the right direction if you are looking for advice.' The food is prepared fresh each day by chef Donald White, husband of manager Elaine. The café offers home-baked scones, cakes, puddings and a lunchtime menu with a vegetarian choice. It is all very reasonably priced – for example, when we visited we enjoyed a filling main meal of pasta, coffee, cold drinks and a delicious and substantial pudding. The bill came to just £9.05 for two. The café is attached to a shop selling fairly traded Third World goods, and all the teas and coffees served in the café are ethically produced. Doves is open Monday to Friday from 10am to 2pm.

Frances Warneford

Two other splendid Cumbrian church cafés are mentioned in this book, and whilst cathedral restaurants did not come within the scope of this research, The Priory at Carlisle Cathedral is well worth a visit.

Way Inn

The Way Inn Christian Centre is strategically placed in the High Street of **Berkhamsted** in Hertfordshire. It all started in Churches Together Lenten Groups discussing the possibility of pioneering a united project in the town. The result is a Post Office, coffee shop and bookshop managed by an ecumenical body of trustees including Anglicans, Baptists, Methodists and Roman Catholics. The name, Way Inn, was borrowed from an earlier ecumenical activity in Berkhamsted when, during a week of evangelism, 'Way In' was an evening venue for teenagers.

The vision statement reads as follows:

> *The Way Inn Christian Centre is a Charitable Trust, set up by members of the Christian Churches in Berkhamsted. The Trust will run the Post Office and stationers through a Limited Company, and there will be a coffee shop where people of the town can drop in for high quality tea and coffee, home-made food, a friendly atmosphere and a listening ear. All profits will go to the Charitable Trust, giving us more opportunities to serve the community of Berkhamsted.*

The stationery area is now called The Book Shop, and the number of Christian books, CDs, tapes and videos sold is rising. This is regarded as an important aspect of the work and witness of the Centre. The coffee shop is in fact a full-blown (but unlicensed) restaurant at lunchtime and whilst it attracts people of all ages there is a steady clientele of elderly people who come for their one hot meal of the day.

For those who need to talk Way Inn provides a confidential counselling service through trained and qualified people to help those struggling with difficult situations ranging from bereavement, marriage, divorce or unemployment to depression and feelings of inadequacy.

With each menu there is the offer of a listening ear, a personal prayer partner and prayer requests to be referred to the Way Inn Prayer Group.

It is worth noting that the Post Office was not part of the original plan, but after two years searching for premises when the existing Post Office became available with the potential for development, it seemed to be the only way to get the project off the ground. 'God moves in a mysterious way ...' If the Trustees had not had the Post Office as a financial backstop in the early days the project would have been bankrupt in about a year. It has now been going for eleven and a half years and even though it will take a few more years to pay off loans and mortgage, it is financially viable.

The Lyttleton Well

Fifteen churches, of all denominations, are united in this work in **Malvern**. Lyttleton Well evolved from the vision of a few people who felt that God was calling them to develop a Christian Centre in the heart of Malvern. In 1993 the centre was opened.

Malvern is famous for its wells and water. The Lyttleton Well recalls the story recorded in St John's Gospel chapter 4 of Jesus meeting a Samaritan woman by Jacob's well. At that well the every-day physical needs of people for water were provided. It was there also that Jesus met the woman's deeper spiritual need. So too, the Lyttleton Well aims to meet the needs of the whole person. The project symbol is of a woman carrying a pitcher.

There are four main aspects to the Well:

1 A COFFEE HOUSE provides simple but good quality food, in a welcoming atmosphere. It is well patronised, and is known as a good and friendly place to be.

2 A CHRISTIAN BOOKSHOP provides a wide range of books, cards and tapes. There is also a RESOURCE CENTRE serving local churches. Apart from the pastoral opportunities of the Coffee House and Bookshop, they also provide the main income for the running of the Well. About 130 volunteers are involved.

3 A COMMUNITY CENTRE, with two halls and smaller rooms, is the venue for a whole variety of community related activities - drop-ins, support groups, lunch club, nursery school, Christian meetings, lettings, charity fund-raising events etc.

4 A COUNSELLING SERVICE offers Christian counselling, by trained counsellors, in a sympathetic and strictly confidential atmosphere.

cuppacare

This venture in **Shipley** began in 1986 under the auspices of Shipley for Christ, which is now called Shipley Churches Together and comprises fourteen congregations of various denominations. For most of the sixteen years it has been housed in the hall of Shipley Baptist Church New Kirkgate, near the Market Square and a short walking distance from the New World Heritage site, Soltaire Village. Initially it was called Shipley for Christ Friendship Centre, but this was too cumbersome and it was renamed Cuppacare as an amalgam of cuppa (for a homely cup of tea or coffee) and care (for the obvious reason). This fitted better on to the external signboard with the cup and cross logo.

The menu is simple, but satisfying; hardly anyone asks for greater variety and the helpers can work efficiently with a limited range of options (filled rolls, scones, orange drink, tea, coffee and biscuits, all at very moderate prices). Refreshments are given free to homeless and other deserving customers. First on the menu is 'Joys and woes shared FREE' and the café motto is: 'We're not fund-raising, we're faith-raising.'

Prices are low and have only been increased twice since 1986! Despite this, about £1,000 a year is given to Christian missions and other causes nominated twice-yearly by the helpers.

The spiritual dimension is catered for as follows:

1 A time of study and prayer is held by the helpers prior to each session. Request slips handed in by customers and helpers form the basis of the prayers.

2 Christian books and greetings cards are sold on the bookstall and free literature supplied by Scripture Gift Mission is offered to interested customers.

3 Counselling is offered to troubled customers (several of whom have been introduced to local churches as a result).

4 The helpers have an annual 'away day' at a chapel in the Yorkshire Dales, with an invited speaker. In this way they get to know each other better and refresh their vision for the work.

The café is child friendly and there is a stock of toys for customers' children to play with.

A bishop from North America was invited to Cuppacare by the local clergyman with whom he was staying. As he entered, he went over to the bookstall manager and said, 'I understand care, but what does cuppa mean?' Most people seem to understand what is on offer and return time after time to savour the friendly atmosphere and, hopefully, the witness offered in the heart of a busy community.

Faith in Exeter

The café at the **Palace Gate Centre** was started in 1979 by South Street Baptist Church and is now part of the ecumenical project at Palace Gate.

The story begins thirty years ago when the city centre churches became acutely aware that homelessness and deprivation are not confined to London, but present in pretty and historical places such as Exeter. The café was South Street's response to this challenge and provided a haven for lonely and vulnerable people. It was one of many community projects envisaged, but the premises did not provide a suitable base, with the church on one street and the hall around a corner.

In 1976 a former wine warehouse and bottling factory was purchased at the back of the church on Palace Gate. The late Bernard Shorland, who was Church Secretary at the time, saw the possibility of linking the warehouse and the church and creating a complex to serve the church's vision for city centre ministry. Bernard's enthusiasm is remembered by the Revd John Stroud who in 1977 was considering an invitation to be South Street's minister. Bernard led him into a wilderness of dust, cobwebs and empty bottles behind the church and as he did so expressed his vision:

'Here in this corner we shall have the kitchen and here will be a room for people to meet in ...' Needless to say, Bernard's enthusiasm was contagious, John Stroud accepted the invitation and was to be part of an evolving venture for nearly twenty years.

Buying the warehouse was one thing, putting it to use quite another. Dirty and derelict, it was also the only place available for all the activities that had been held in the church hall which was sold to the Shillhay Community to be used as a hostel for thirty homeless men. By the summer of 1979 the work was completed of bringing together the warehouse and the re-ordered, now multi-purpose church, with only glass doors separating the worship area from coffee shop, luncheon club, day centre for the elderly, play group and all the other activities that over the years would find a home at the Palace Gate Centre.

Anglican churches in the city were also engaged in community outreach and in 1991 they joined with the Baptists to start The Palace Gate Project. With the support of Government grants and assistance from the Church Urban Fund, professional staff were appointed to work with the volunteers. It is an ongoing development including a furniture project, drop-in and counselling services, Christmas Care and Food Voucher Scheme, ministry to the homeless and to discharged prisoners.

Through all the changing scenes, the café has remained a haven. One customer described it as: 'The only restaurant in Exeter where you can sit for four hours without being asked to order anything.'

Change and Renewal

Buildings are a resource of the Christian Church. Isaac Watts recognised this when he wrote:

> These temples of His grace,
> How beautiful they stand!
> The honours of our native place,
> And bulwarks of our land.

Winston Churchill said, 'We shape our buildings and then our buildings shape us.' Often that is true and many a battle is still fought between fixed pews and flexible chairs. In this section you can read about fires that proved to be blessings in disguise, redundancy followed by resurrection clothing dry bones with new flesh, and the response to a major tragedy shaping the function of a building.

Henry Francis Lyte's well-known hymn, 'Abide with Me', speaks about, 'Change and decay in all around I see'. Thankfully 'change and decay' are not indissolubly joined together. There are miracles of transformation spelling change and renewal ...

All Saints
Leighton Buzzard

The builders of All Saints certainly knew where to position a church. Approach Leighton Buzzard from any direction and you will see the thirteenth-century spire. It's not the spire but the fire that sends shivers through many who were worshippers at All Saints in the 1980s. On 13 April 1985 a huge mystery blaze caused two million pounds worth of damage to this fine building.

The church had no hall and thought had previously been given to developing the south side to provide more accommodation. Such a scheme was considered to be impractical. The fire gave a new opportunity for the Church Council to look again at what could be done.

Terry Warburton, who was churchwarden at the time, writes:

It may sound fanciful, but it is nonetheless true, the answer came in a dream. I imagined walking through a window space in the north transept and down a corridor into what was then the medieval clergy vestry. Dividing the high north transept into two, horizontally and building a matching two storey extension linking the transept with the vestry would meet our needs. It would be separately heated too. I nudged my wife awake to tell her! It would provide six rooms, more toilets – and space for a coffee area and bookstall.

With the encouragement of the then vicar, I assembled a small group to progress the idea and plans were prepared for the Church Council. The report proposed that, 'The new accommodation would be self sufficient, even to the extent of a separate heating system ... perhaps a rota of volunteers could be drawn up to open the coffee area on weekdays and Saturdays – a far more attractive proposition if the rooms are warm and properly equipped.'

And it came to pass ... the Council accepted the plans which were passed to the architect for his attention. About this time a faithful elderly member of the congregation died and left her house to the church. The money from this sale, combined with the church's own reserves, just covered the cost.

The church has always attracted visitors. Before the fire, the best hospitality which could occasionally be offered was instant coffee from an urn on a table in the north transept. A matching cup and saucer was a triumph! Now the Coffee Shop, seating 24 and with extra space in an adjacent room at busy times, has cloths and flowers on the tables and attractive china! A major disaster has enabled the church to take a giant leap forward.

St Nicholas Centre
Whitehaven

In the year 1663 Whitehaven was a hamlet of nine houses, but as a result of developing coal resources in the area and people finding employment in the mines, the population had increased to two thousand by 1693. In that year the Church of St Nicholas was consecrated to replace a very small building dating back to 1642. In 1883 a new St Nicholas was built of red sandstone with accommodation for a thousand when required. Buried in St Nicholas' churchyard is Mildred Warner Gale, the grandmother of George Washington, first President of the United States of America. Mildred's second marriage was to George Gale, a Merchant of Whitehaven.

On the afternoon of 31 August 1971 the nave and the sanctuary were completely destroyed by fire. Two years later it was decided not to rebuild and the congregation which had been worshipping in the interim with Christ Church was united as the Parish Church of Christ Church/St Nicholas in 1974. Later it joined with St James' to be the Parish of Whitehaven. By 1987 the St Nicholas tower area had been refurbished providing an area for worship, a meeting/display space, kitchen, toilet, storage and office facilities. The Centre has become a busy welcoming meeting place for both the local community and visitors to the town. Refreshments are served to about 1,300 people a week by enthusiastic volunteers. Other organisations, churches and charities staff the café on Saturdays.

The chapel is separated from the coffee area by a beautifully engraved glass screen with doors that open up to include the whole floor when more chapel area is needed. Into the building has been built an extra floor of light oak, reached by an open stairway of parana pine and redwood. The floor is two level, one given over to a Parish Office and Resources Centre providing material for schools, Sunday schools and youth groups, the other provides an area of overflow to the refreshment area downstairs or a meeting/exhibitions space.

In a town that owed much of its development to the coal mining industry, it is fitting that there should be a lasting tribute to the workers who lost their lives in the pits. There are two such memorials in St Nicholas' grounds. The one that is near the entrance from Duke Street is inscribed with the names of the children who died while working underground. A book by a local ex-miner, Ray Devlin, called *The Children of the Pits*, gives a very graphic account of working conditions at that time. The second memorial is in the former nave area. This is a mosaic of a pit wheel and each part illustrates a connection with mining. The spokes of the wheel bear the names of pits that have operated in the Whitehaven district from 1597 until the last one closed in 1986. Red and yellow stones repre-

sent heat and power, while green slate strips form the sea. The centre of the mosaic shows the Edward Medal, which is awarded in cases of bravery to rescuers who risk their own lives, to recover both the living and the dead in the aftermath of a pit accident.

Set in its award-winning gardens, St Nicholas Centre has proved to be 'a phoenix that rose from the ashes'.

Lantern Light Rekindled

ICHABOD ('The Glory is departed,' 1 Samuel 4.21) would be an appropriate word to describe Raynes Park Methodist Church, **Wimbledon** in the early 1990s. This enormous red brick building was in a poor state of repair and a drain on the resources of the congregation. A church with a glorious past was at a low ebb, 'the shine had been knocked off the ball', but the light from the lantern on top of the church still spread over the neighbourhood during the hours of darkness. The lantern was eventually to become the symbol of rebirth.

Rodney Hill, who became minister of the church in 1993, was greeted by a wonderfully gifted team of people fully aware of the problems, but willing to work in partnership with him. Soon there was a vision for the future and through prayer, fund-raising, imagination and sheer hard work the premises have been transformed to become the servant of the church's mission in the local community. This includes the Lantern Arts Centre encouraging the use of drama, creative writing, dance, visual arts and music in worship and in the area of individual spiritual development.

One of the major fund-raising efforts was a monthly market held on the fourth Saturday of the month with about a dozen stalls. In the centre of the hall, tables and chairs were set up for teas and coffees to be served. Many of those who came to the market were not members of the church, but they bought bits and pieces and made friends over a drink and chat. The market had become a valuable meeting place and confirmed research already made that a coffee shop was needed in the area.

The idea was further explored at an open meeting for anyone interested from all the churches in Raynes Park. More than fifty people representing six different churches, from Free Evangelical through to Roman Catholic, came to hear about the possibility and there was

137

considerable interest and enthusiasm. A steering group was formed to develop the concept of a coffee shop to be built between the hall and the church. In April 1996 it was opened with the aim of providing refreshment, a listening ear and company for the lonely, making a visible statement to the community that the church had changed.

From the busy main road passers-by see the sign to the **Lantern Coffee Shop**. The interior is bright with attractive tableware and glass doors opening on to a quiet Bible Garden. There is a Christian bookstall and Traidcraft goods are sold. It hosts a regular Luncheon Club offering a four-course meal for the elderly – keenly attended by around 40 local people. They've also been invited to 'activity sessions' to try their hand at crafts and flower-arranging. The Toddlers Group is especially welcomed by single and disadvantaged parents. Regular collections of food and bedding are made for asylum seekers, in liaison with local refugee organisations.

There is a Key Worker who co-ordinates the various activities of the Lantern Project which also depends on a number of volunteers. Some come from other churches in the area. Others have come via Merton Volunteer Bureau. Change and renewal with the Lantern light shining even more brightly.

More Than a Pinch of Salt in Oldham

When the Salt Cellar in Oldham celebrated its tenth anniversary in the Millennium Year, it was estimated that 750,000 people had been served in two buildings converted into restaurants.

In this multi-ethnic northern town in the heart of Lancashire, once famous for its cotton mills, Methodists had for years experienced a sense of loss and failure and eventually force of circumstances combined to leave the town centre devoid of a Methodist presence. When the Revd Wesley Cook was appointed Superintendent Minister in 1985 he inspired a new vision for ministry and mission. Soon he had people dreaming their own dreams and exploring together the possibility of re-entering the town with a fresh image and approach. Members of the Oldham and Saddleworth Circuit Meeting affirmed their commitment to turn dreams into reality and the process of looking for premises began. A property on Church Lane near the Market Place became available, not only was the address number 10, but it belonged to:

Number 10 was purchased and in the spring and summer of 1990 the three-storey building was transformed into a restaurant with counselling rooms and a Christian Resources Centre. Wesley Cook asked people to choose a name for this new venture. Many suggested 'Salt Cellar' and this was adopted. There was an immediate impact on the town and the church quickly discovered a new role, not only serving drinks, snacks and three-course meals to between three and four thousand people a week, but also offering the wider hospitality of friendship and support. The volunteers, initially drawn from churches in the area, built up to a rota of 150, including many of the regular customers.

After being open five years, Number 10 was not big enough for this growing enterprise. The search was now on for larger premises. It was often said that the County Court Building opposite would be ideal and much to everybody's surprise, just at the right time, it came on to the market to be sold by auction. The offer had to be a sealed bid to an office in Manchester and whoever offered the highest bid would succeed in obtaining the building. The funding for the purchase was arranged and the bid was successful. In the summer of 1998 a second building conversion was underway and by November, the new Salt Cellar was open.

The spacious restaurant is on two levels downstairs. The tables and chairs are sensitive to the building's old grandeur. Whilst always busy, it manages to retain a warm, friendly and relaxed atmosphere. There is a lift to other floors accommodating counselling facilities, meeting rooms and Number 1 Court is now a multi-purpose worship area.

The outreach of the Salt Cellar continues to evolve with a variety of ministries, including a Youth Project and Street Evangelism, resulting in 'more than a pinch of salt' flavouring the life of Oldham.

A Vibrant New Heart for Walsall

Standing at the busy crossroads of life in Walsall town centre, near to the bus station and post office, stands St Paul's Church. This Gothic-style building was erected in 1826 replacing the Chapel of Queen Mary's School (the school founded by Mary Tudor in 1554). The first vicar used the church to provide soup kitchens and medical services for the community.

By the 1960s the area around St Paul's had changed from residential to commercial and redundancy threatened the building. Plans to sell the site for the building of a supermarket met with a public outcry. Eventually church members explored a vision to develop a new style of ministry throughout the week in partnership with the local community. To facilitate this change, the church was redeveloped in 1994/5 and the whole building is now known as **The Crossing at St Paul's** or St Paul's Church at the Crossing.

From the outside the building may look near enough the same as it has done for the last century, but inside a spectacular change has taken place which has turned it into a multi-level complex. The ground floor consists of seven retail units which celebrate arts and crafts, fashion and flowers, books, gifts and music. The Day Chapel

THE CROSSING
AT SAINT PAULS

Ground Floor
and Mezzanine

is open to all from Monday to Saturday, 8.30 a.m. to 5.30 p.m., for private prayer and quiet reflection.

The first floor includes a restaurant, which provides quality food at competitive prices in an uplifting, smoke-free environment. This level also includes the office of Walsall Carers' Trust, the Centre Manager's Office and the offices of St Paul's Church, where a Church of England priest is usually available. The second floor is used for worship by St Paul's Church at 10.30 a.m. every Sunday. The meeting area and ancillary rooms are also used for a wide variety of functions, including conferences, training events, exhibitions and concerts. 'The Crossing' refers to the meeting point of church and community, as well as to the crossing over from death to new life which is central to Christian faith.

The Crossing banner, depicted in the hangings over the shopping mall and in stained glass in the doors on the first floor balcony, combines a striking series of Christian symbols:

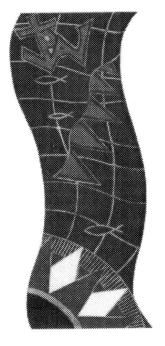

- *The logo of St Paul's Church.* In Ancient Greek tradition, the letters of a name were turned back to front or disguised in some way and then combined with a significant symbol to form a monogram. In this case the name 'Paul' is combined with a Latin Cross. This logo is also set into the floor of the shopping mall, under the Light Well Cross.
- *The Net.* Jesus once introduced a parable in these words: 'The Kingdom of God is like a net,' which suggests that there is room for all sorts of different people to be gathered into its capacious embrace.
- *The Fish.* The Greek word for fish (Icthus) provides the initial letters of the Greek for 'Jesus Christ, Son of God, Saviour.'

- *The Compass* is about creation and God's concern for the whole of life.
- *The Bunting* represents a centre of celebration which is the aim of this whole project in the centre of Walsall.

These are all elements important in the work of The Crossing with worship at its heart.

The Crossing at St Paul's provides for a wide range of needs within the local community including a pre-school education child-care unit. The restaurant offers a variety of food from breakfast, through to lunches and afternoon tea, and is also able to cater for meetings, functions, Christmas dinners and children's parties.

A striking new feature on the outside is the glass lantern at the apex of the roof, sitting above the light well and allowing sunlight to illuminate the fine, original roof structure and pour down through the light wells in the newly inserted floors. A seventy-foot-high cross made of pieces of sculpted safety glass, stacked on metal rods and weighing almost a ton hangs as a feature in the light well. This was designed by the American artist, Danny Lane. The symbol of the cross unites the work of The Crossing on all three floors expressing God's interest in the whole of life. The four horizontal arms of the cross point north, south, east and west symbolising the ministry of Christ, reaching out to all.

The Spurriergate Centre

The Church of St Michael's Spurriergate is situated in the heart of the historic city of **York**. The church is an Anglican building with features dating back to the twelfth century.

The building ceased to be a church, in the traditional sense, in the mid-1970s when it was declared redundant. It was closed to the public for a number of years and the Diocese approached the Parochial Church Council of St Michael le Belfrey regarding its future.

In October 1989 the Spurriergate Centre was opened to the public after significant redevelopment as a space for rest, relaxation and gentle Christian witness. During the thirteen years since, it has gained a reputation for being supportive and welcoming on many different levels.

The Centre's mission is to share God's love with the people of York and its visitors through caring service in the restaurant and shop; to encourage justice in trading - in the price, quality and origin of the goods sold; to offer a listening ear; to share the Good News of Jesus Christ.

The Centre opens to the public from Monday to Saturday and serves freshly made quality food and drink throughout the day. There are full-time and voluntary staff - most going to local churches of various denominations - but also some staff who wouldn't describe themselves as active Christians. The Centre sees about 3,000 people through the premises per week from all walks of life and has received a number of awards for the quality of its food, child friendliness and innovation in 'social' commerce.

There are also two retail spaces within the Centre that sell cards, gifts and other small products - the majority of which are fairly traded. These commercial activities provide the funding to support pastoral work both in the building itself and within the local community. In the annex of the Centre there is a fully professional counselling service available each day.

Customers are invited to submit written prayer requests which are prayed through at the informal service held daily at 9.30 a.m. During times of local or national crisis, Spurriergate has become a place where people feel safe to express their feelings. The Centre positively encourages such expression and also provides a small chapel space within the building.

The Spurriergate Centre had a major reshape in 1999 to reflect the change in 'coffee culture' in the city. This £70,000 scheme resulted in **The Cloisters** – an upper deck with comfortable casual furniture, Danish pastries and cappuccino coffee.

St Sampson's

St Sampson's was a redundant church in the centre of **York**. It is now a meeting place and social centre for anyone over sixty. This ancient church was built in the fourteenth and fifteenth centuries and is one of very few dedicated to St Sampson, a sixth-century bishop connected with Wales, South West England, Brittany and Guernsey.

Mounting costs and dwindling congregations made it impossible to maintain St Sampson's as a parish church in the market area of York and in 1968 it was closed. Various schemes to convert it for other uses failed and there was a distinct possibility that it may have to be demolished. Eventually the York Civic Trust took it over and with the help of gifts and grants it was re-opened in November 1974 as a social centre for the over 60s. The use of the building has gone full circle because when first built it would have been very much a community centre and not just for Sunday worship. The medieval churches in York were used as schools, courtrooms, meeting halls and even as places for transacting business deals. Now St Sampson's is a community centre once more and in that role has taken on a new lease of life.

The adjoining derelict parish hall was acquired and transformed to give extra space and part of the old churchyard is now an attractive garden. A small chapel has been preserved containing some of the original furnishings. A service is held here each Wednesday at noon. Next to the chapel is a reading room with daily newspapers and a library of books which can be borrowed. In addition to the daily restaurant facilities there is a monthly dance, an over-sixties choir, coach trips and a monthly magazine called *Senior Voices*. Over 1,000 people are attracted to the centre each day and visitors come from the UK and many other countries. Sixty Plus is the one qualification for entry.

All Saints

In the centre of **Hereford** a church that a few years ago was about to be declared redundant and boarded up has become a centre for celebrating human creativity in all its forms. All Saints seeks to bring the holy into the ordinary and the ordinary into the holy.

Delicious fresh food is served at fair prices. Everything is made in the kitchen each day (including the bread for sandwiches which is baked by the staff). Whether eaten in the café or taken away, just a cappuccino and a cake or a full meal, the staff aim to serve in an efficient and friendly manner.

The building provides a wonderful resource for music and drama, recitals and exhibitions. All Saints is keen to promote and encourage the very best of human creativity by providing a central venue for such productions or exhibitions.

Just as the medieval churches were places where a lot more than worship happened, so too All Saints is a place where there is a lot going on and the divisions between sacred and secular are broken down. In the nave and south chapel just about anything can happen from talks to sales, meetings to lunches.

Underlying all that All Saints does is a rhythm of worship. Silence in the Lady Chapel, weekday Evening Prayer, the midday Eucharist or the Sung Mass on Sunday all provide opportunities to worship God. Central to worshipping life is the Eucharist, the Holy Communion, the Great Thanksgiving, where God's love for us in Jesus is revealed in the breaking of bread and sharing of wine. Joining together in worship is a communal act of praise and thanksgiving to God our Creator and serves to encourage and support the Christian community in this place.

TREASURE FROM TRAGEDY

First on the Scene

The Salvation Army had a presence in **Lockerbie** until 1939, around this time the corps closed and the area was covered from the nearby town of Annan.

On 21 December 1988 this small town suddenly and tragically hit the headlines when a Pan-Am jet crashed there killing 270 people. The Salvation Army was the first voluntary organisation to arrive on the scene. Initially the majority of help offered by the Salvation Army was of a practical nature, food, blankets, mortuary duty etc. This gradually progressed to a counselling service, which remained active for over two years following the tragedy.

The counselling ministry 'opened eyes' to the possibility of establishing a more permanent work in the town. Rather unusually the first initiative was the opening of a small charity shop. This was rented and occupied approximately half the area which is currently used as the café. The warmth of the people and the success of this venture led to the Salvation Army purchasing the whole building in which the charity shop operated and in 1993 **The Coffee Pot** opened followed by the Salvation Army Corps (church).

The Coffee Pot

The purpose of the Coffee Pot was to provide an informal, relaxed atmosphere where people could purchase reasonably priced food and, if desired, share in conversation.

A number of links with members of the community were made and this led to some of these people attending the services. Indeed some of them have since come to faith and become active members of the church.

Vital Links

I am frequently asked at the Buxton Church, 'How does our café compare with those you have visited?' My reply is always the same, 'It's perfect.' It fulfils the intention for which it was started over thirty years ago to provide soup, drinks and toast for shoppers, market-stall holders and visitors to the town. The welcome poster outside simply says, PEOPLE MEET PEOPLE IN OUR CAFÉ. For many it is the local rendezvous for meeting friends and catching up with the latest news. Since the Vision 2000 Development Scheme the building has become a community resource and groups using the premises discover the café. Following the Tuesday Morning Service it provides a meeting place for extended fellowship.

All the cafés listed have an intention to fulfil, sometimes briefly summarised in a written mission or vision statement. Vital links between church and community vibrate through the Directory and in profiles already included in the different sections of this book. Cafés are often set in the context of other church-sponsored community projects. (Bath, Belfast, Newcastle and Portsmouth are used as illustrations.) Sometimes a valuable project is facilitated by a church offering premises and collaborating with other bodies (e.g. Nibbles at Claremont). Many vital links are made through listening to what a community is saying. (The cafés at Old Basing and in the Fairfield area of Buxton are a direct result of neighbourhood surveys.) The challenge to 'think globally and act locally' brings another dimension into the life of church cafés and this section concludes with an emphasis on fair trading.

Bath
Manvers Street Baptist Church

The church weekly notice sheet welcomes 'all who wish to explore the Christian faith and live out its purpose for our city and world today'. There follows a list of activities headed 'The Church at Work and Worship'. Central to everything is the vision of the church as an open house. The delightful restaurant, open Monday to Saturday, serving hot meals, snacks and home-made cakes and pastries is part of

It all began a number of years ago when Elsie was in the church arranging flowers. She noticed parents waiting in the basement for their children to emerge from the Saturday morning dance class. Elsie suggested to her fellow deacons at the time that they refurbish the old coffee bar, no longer in use, and offer at least a cup of coffee or tea to those using the church premises. A small group met to initiate the project and soon a coffee shop was opened. The profits from this small beginning helped to furnish the new Open House, six-days-a-week coffee shop, which had always been Elsie's vision for this town centre church near to both the railway and bus stations.

There are many coffee shops in Bath. This one exists because Christians have heard God's call to serve, to care, and to exercise the gift of hospitality. It is one among many ministries of the Open House Centre:

* *The Baby and Toddler Group.* A friendly, relaxing place for parents, carers and their youngsters. A team of people from across the generations provides a lively, thriving setting for folk to make new friends in a safe and stimulating environment.

- *Julian House.* A night shelter and day centre operated by Bath Churches Housing Association all year round for men and women, helping them to fulfil their own expectations.
- *Off the Record.* A Youth Advice, Information and Counselling Centre with full-time staff and trained volunteers; providing a confidential non-directive support for young people on a 'walk-in' basis.

Recently the Church Worship Centre has been transformed and in addition to Sunday worship there is a pause for thought and reflection each Tuesday at 1.10 p.m. Traidcraft products and all the Iona Wild Goose Publications are available in the bookshop.

Paradise in Bath: the before and after effect

A large board has appeared outside Manvers Street Baptist Church at Bath proclaiming 'Paradise'. It is not, as might be supposed, a sudden affirmation by members of the church, but a builders' board designed to inform passers by that work has begun on the redecoration and refurbishment of the church by the appropriately named H. J. Paradise and Sons.

It is hoped that the work will be completed by the autumn and a time of celebration and commitment is planned for the first weekend in October.

'The double meaning of the sign has already raised a few smiles,' says senior minister the Revd John Rackley. 'The challenge is what sort of advertisement will we be when the Paradise board is removed? There is unlikely to be any playing of harps or flapping of wings, but hopefully renewed enthusiasm for this island of light in the centre of Bath.'

Baptist Times, 9 August 2001

The Scallop Shell
Belfast

The scallop shell is a sign of pilgrimage and part of the Wesley coat of arms. In the centre of Belfast at Grosvenor House, the headquarters of the Methodist Central Mission, the coffee shop is called

The Scallop Shell. The Mission was founded in 1889 to meet the challenge of social needs within the city. 'Need not Creed' was the motto of its founder, the Revd Crawford Johnson, and under that banner the work of the Mission continues today with its wide range of projects expressing the Christian Faith in Action through professional social outreach.

- *Advice Centre, Belfast.* Inner-city support centre for people in distress. Includes annual cross-community holiday programmes for children and senior citizens.
- *Anderson House, Newtownards, Bangor and Belfast.* Supported housing for young adults preparing to live independently in the community.
- *Childhaven Centre, Millisle.* Venue for BCM's holiday programmes and multi-purpose facility for the whole community.
- *Craigmore House and Marmion, Millisle and Holywood.* Residential units for young people aged twelve to eighteen.
- *Kirk House, Belfast.* Residential care for older people.
- *The Quayside Project, Newtownards.* Care in the community for young people and families.

At the heart of it all are three congregations in different parts of the city. Sandy Row, Springfield Road and Grosvenor House opened in 1997 to replace the former Central Hall and as a new facility for the millennium for the people of Belfast and beyond.

Located in the Golden Mile area of the city, it includes a multi-purpose hall, the Gallagher Chapel named after a former minister, the Advice Centre, ancillary rooms, administration centre and the Conference and Training Centre.

On the ground floor is the street-front Scallop Shell Coffee Shop, offering a warm welcome and varied menu at highly competitive prices from Monday to Friday each week.

The hundreds of pilgrims who make their way to The Scallop Shell at Grosvenor House appreciate the lovely atmosphere, are served by friendly staff and enjoy good food.

Newcastle

Brunswick Methodist Church in Newcastle has direct links with John Wesley who first visited the city in May 1742 and made it his northern headquarters for riding back and forth into the North-East and Scotland. In Newcastle he built an Orphan House which was also a school, library, bookshop, hostel and preaching house. When the work began to thrive in the North-East and the Orphan House became too small,

 Brunswick Chapel was opened in 1821 with seating for 1,600 people.

Over 150 years later the premises were modernised. In the 1970s a new floor was constructed at gallery level providing a reduced amount of worship space on the first floor and downstairs is the base for community work including a hall, kitchen, meeting rooms, offices and a large foyer in which the **Sandwich Bar** operates and is one of three major projects sponsored by the church.

The Listening Post is a Christian-based organisation which sets out to be available and accessible to anyone who may need it. About 2,000 people a year with diverse and complex needs come from all over the region. The twenty-seventh Annual Report in 2001 contained this relevant information:

The constant attitude of openness and a ready welcome is provided by a team of 35 Listeners, ordinary people of all ages and from all walks of life, each having their own special quality to offer, but all dedicated to the work of listening, believing that it is a worthwhile service to give. When accepted after training on to the rota for listening, the volunteers agree to commit themselves to one-and-a-half hours per week or three hours per fortnight. This means that at present we are only able to have two Listeners instead of three on each session. We have a very small stand-by list of Listeners who fill in for sickness and holidays. Our Listeners are drawn from the congregations of churches throughout Northumberland and Tyne & Wear.

The Mission Statement of the **Brunswick Young People's Project** outlines its vision:

Brunswick Young People's Project is based in the city centre of Newcastle and works with young people, aged 16-25, to counterbalance the effects of poverty, unemployment, homelessness and discrimination in its widest terms. This is achieved through city centre detached youth work, the provision of a drop-in and the establishing and encouraging of individual and group support. Brunswick Young People's Project is founded on the fundamental principles that underpin youth work. As a project we believe that work with young people is a process of informal education, both political and social. The rationale for this approach is to empower young people, allowing them to take appropriate choices and gain greater control over the decisions affecting their lives.

The project worked with over 800 young people last year, responding to a variety of needs, and 'The Independent Living Course' was featured in the *Guardian* newspaper. Some of the young people involved are quoted in the Annual Report.

I've been coming to Brunswick Young People's Project for quite a long time and still find their support very helpful. The workers help you in emotional and practical ways. – DAWN

I've been here in Newcastle about six months. I was homeless when I arrived here, but now I'm in a better position. The Brunswick Young People's Project is a place where you can chill-out. The people who come here have various problems and a lot in common with each other. Talking to and meeting new people has helped in many ways. – GARY

The minister of the church, the Revd Terry Hurst, says: 'John Wesley's first contribution to eighteenth-century Newcastle was an Orphan House; his twentieth-century followers envisioned a new way to carry on his work; we in the twenty-first century have the privilege to continue it.' The Sandwich Bar serves 1,000 people a week. The bread buns have mouth-watering fillings. Listening Post and Brunswick Young People's Project affirm that we do not live by bread alone!

The Haven
A community centre
serving the people of Landport.

> While women weep as they do now, I'll fight; while little children
> go hungry as they do now, I'll fight; while men go to prison, in
> and out, in and out, I'll fight; while there is a poor lost girl upon
> the street, I'll fight; while there yet remains one dark soul without
> the light of God, I'll fight – I'll fight to the very end.

These words were spoken by General William Booth who founded
the Salvation Army in 1878.

In a series of articles on 'Spirituality Today' Dr John Newton, a
Methodist minister, refers to one popular description of the
Salvation Army as: 'Christianity with its Sleeves Rolled Up'. Dr
Newton continues:

> William Booth knew poverty experientially from his own upbring-
> ing and he never lost his passionate concern to bring the benefits
> of the Gospel to the poorest of the poor. That spirit still animates
> the Salvation Army. Its pioneering social work – in hospitals,
> orphanages, day centres, refuges, night shelters – has developed
> into a highly efficient form of community service. Yet its concern
> for salvation, for men and women brought to the new life in
> Christ, remains central. It is, 'Whole Salvation', not an attenuated
> 'Soul Salvation' that the Army offers in Jesus' name.

The Haven puts flesh on these words. It is an integral part of the
Portsmouth Citadel Corps of the Salvation Army and is open six
days a week and comprises a restaurant, a fully equipped kitchen, a
charity shop, two nurseries and a furniture store. The centre opened
in June 1994 and has cost in excess of half a million pounds to
construct. The area around the centre contains a mixture of post-war
flats and modern new housing: these not only accommodate a considerable concentration of people, they also represent much social

deprivation and need. In this inner city area are all the signs of a community in crisis; high levels of unemployment, broken homes, single parent families and petty crime are common place. Since it is people that shape the society we live in, serving people is at the heart of the work undertaken by The Haven community centre. The few full-time staff are wonderfully assisted by some three dozen volunteers in any week of activities. The many and varied activities demonstrate practical Christianity in action.

The restaurant is open to the public from Monday to Saturday each week serving a variety of low cost meals and snacks. A wide ranging menu with a choice of two main course dishes is available daily and around 400 hot meals are served weekly. In addition a Meals-on-Wheels service, run in conjunction with Social Services, provides meals delivered to elderly and disabled people in the centre of Portsmouth. Some 250 freshly cooked meals are delivered each week. A twice weekly luncheon club for senior citizens meets on the premises. In addition to all this the centre offers a qualified hairdresser for men, women and children at very reasonable prices.

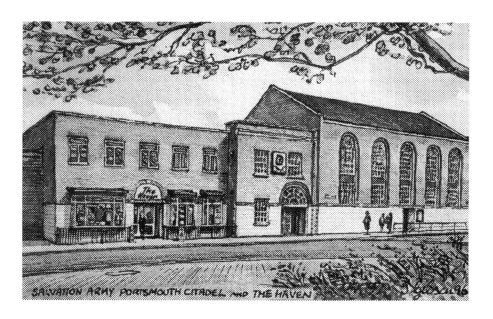

SALVATION ARMY PORTSMOUTH CITADEL AND THE HAVEN

Bathing services are available, staffed if required, by caring volunteers. This facility, incorporating a hydraulic chair lift, is particularly aimed at the elderly and disabled. The Good Neighbours project aims to identify senior members of the community who, with a little help, can live with independence in their own homes. Both full-time staff and volunteers help in visiting and befriending, collection of prescriptions and shopping, small repairs and practical help. The charity shop stocks a continually changing supply of good quality clothing, shoes, toys, bric-a-brac, small items of furniture and books. There is also a furniture shop where furniture supplied through generous public donations is displayed and sold at low cost to the general public. The furniture shop also works closely with Portsmouth City Council, with whom a contract exists for the supply of furniture to families in extreme difficulty and need. The Haven Baby Nursery is for babies aged 6 months to 2 years 9 months and the Haven Nursery is for children aged 2 years 9 months to 5 years. The rooms are light, warm and welcoming, with excellent play facilities and activities include pre-school maths, reading and writing skills, music, art, craft and science – with an emphasis on promoting personal and social proficiency and an awareness of the world about us – which includes daily outings.

A number of young people are employed under the New Deal Welfare to Work Training Scheme – in the kitchen, the nurseries and in the furniture service; a number of people who were engaged on the New Deal Scheme and who served their time as trainees have now been taken on as full-time paid employees.

This project illustrates the changing face of the Salvation Army, but always remaining true to its founder's ethos captured in Fred Pratt Green's words:

> The Church of Christ, in every age
> Beset by change but Spirit-led,
> Must claim and test its heritage
> And keep on rising from the dead.

Reprinted by permission of Stainer & Bell Ltd

nibbles@claremont

Blackpool

Nibbles Café is strongly supported by North Shore Methodist Church in Blackpool but is independent of it.

Claremont First Step Centre is a community centre which is helping to bring a new sense of unity in one of Blackpool's most deprived areas. It opened in June 2000, funded by the Government's Single Regeneration Budget, in beautifully restored rooms at North Shore Church. It provides a base for a variety of community activities from Alcoholics Anonymous meetings to exercise classes. Uniformed youth groups meet there; a thriving community orchestra, the Darby and Joan Club and a playgroup.

It's a base for blood-donor sessions, for a baby milk clinic, Barnardo's parenting classes, the Credit Union, and a mini-market for charity every Wednesday. Poco Loco, a Samba band, sets the rhythm with its weekly meetings. Disability Leisure Link operates from there, and some of its disabled volunteers help staff the reception desk.

The Claremont First Step Centre illustrates the way urban areas can pull together to the benefit of everyone. The aim is to build a sense of community and to enable people to work together. Having a café included is a bonus. It provides a focal point for the centre.

Nibbles is run by a group of eight people with learning difficulties from Langdale Centre, Mereside. Langdale clients who wanted to work in the town centre venture – they don't get paid – had to apply for their jobs and go through a formal interview. They have all gained their food hygiene certificates and are working towards other basic qualifications in food and hospitality. They work as a team, with day centre officers providing guidance on front-of-house and helping with food preparation.

157

For some, the morning starts with a shopping expedition to stock up on anything needed for the day, including fresh bread and salads, while others stay behind to start on laying tables and baking – all cakes and scones are fresh each day. From 10 a.m. onwards, the café is busy. Local residents, people working nearby and holiday-makers drop in for a break.

The menu is deliberately kept simple and has an emphasis on healthy eating – apart from the very tempting cakes – to ensure it doesn't rival the traditional cafés nearby. No fried foods, no main meals and no chips. There is a daily specials board e.g. hummus with pitta bread and Greek salad, sandwiches with a generous side salad and jacket potatoes with a variety of fillings.

Nibbles provides its team with valuable experience in workplace skills which, hopefully, will lead to employment and choices. Working as a team they are involved in menu planning and budgeting as well as preparing food and serving it. One member of the team recently landed a job as a breakfast waiter at a Blackpool hotel. At the moment it is only one day a week for four hours, but at the age of forty-three it marks a huge milestone in his life.

NIBBLES @ CLAREMONT TEAM MEMBERS VIEWS

We all get on well and work as a team. I enjoy my job and get on well with all with the customers. I like helping people and serving them ... I would like to work in the hotel trade. Working here will help me to do this. – DOREEN, *counter-front staff*

I can make the scones and ice the cakes, especially the chocolate cake. Everybody likes my carrot cake. The kitchen is bright ... we make salads. I am learning this for my basic food hygiene and hope to do my NVQ level 1 in catering. – SUSAN, *kitchen staff*

I love cooking and baking cakes, and making salads. We sometimes make pizzas and lasagne. They are my favourites. We make all different things for the specials. I work in the kitchen, but would like to work on the counter. I like baking biscuits for the children in the nursery.   – PAMELA, *kitchen staff*

I like the set out of the building because it looks brand new. I have worked in the kitchen and at the front serving the customers ... I like working on the back and front. I like planning the specials.

I like it because we are separate from everything and we can make our own decisions. Everyone is easy to get on with.

– AMANDA, *counter-front staff*

Le Café Bienvenu
St Mary's Church, Old Basing

The parish of Old Basing is split into two halves, an old and a new. The older part is the village of Old Basing, and the newer area is Lychpit, a large modern housing estate on the north side of the parish. The two areas are joined by road but separated by the Loddon valley open space, a river and a railway line. The inhabitants of the village are typically middle to retirement age, of 'grandparent' age group. Whereas the majority of Lychpit residents are in the thirty to forty-five, 'parent' age group. In the parish as a whole the largest age group is thirty-five to fifty-four followed by children of between five and fourteen years.

At its centre the village has thatched cottages, and a church dating back to 1088. It is a place of considerable historic interest, mentioned in the Domesday Book. Small housing estates were built in the fifties and sixties to the south of the central area. Some people have lived in the village all their lives. Lychpit, on the other hand is a place of

159

transition. It has evolved over the last two decades and now houses many young families and single people who stay for a few years and then move on. Some move into the village which is perceived as more permanent and up-market. Both areas are thought of as being desirable places to live.

The main source of employment in the area is the computer industry and computer-related industries. Many commute to London or work in 'England's Silicon valley' (the Thames valley and the M4 corridor). Long term unemployment is rare although redundancy has been part of many people's experience. People move around within the computer industry fairly frequently which contributes to the mobility of the population. Few have extended family living nearby. The majority of people here own cars and many also have a company car. Most have a very good standard of living although financial problems are not uncommon, especially in families with children.

This is the introduction to a sociological study of her local community by the Revd Kathy O'Loughlin. Kathy is Assistant Priest at St Mary's, Old Basing and the project formed part of her ordination training in 1998. As a mother with three children, she was particularly interested in the experience of motherhood in the parish. Kathy sent four hundred questionnaires out to all mothers whose children attended the local schools (see **Behind the Scenes**).

From the results of the questionnaire, there were three important findings:

1. Mothers in Old Basing have common needs:
   - time and space for themselves
   - support and encouragement
   - contact with other mothers
2. The majority of women who participated in the study do not feel that their needs are being met at present.
3. Eighty-one per cent of respondents thought the church could help to meet these needs.

A 'Feedback Day' was held in the Parish Room when the findings were shared and consideration given to what should be done next. Various options were discussed at length. The outcome was Le Café Bienvenu – a French-style café which opens every Friday during school term time at 8.40 a.m. so that parents can drop their children off at school and then come in for croissant and coffee etc. It closes at about 11.00 a.m. The staff (ten women and one man) all have children at the schools and work on a rota basis. There is a play area for children, but it is not a toddler group. It is attached to the church, but is not a church group. It aims to provide a friendly caring atmosphere where mothers can have a break, but is open to all. It has also generated a great deal of fun. At Easter there are egg-and-spoon races round the outside of the church and all the staff wear bunny ears; at Christmas members of the Parochial Church Council are persuaded to serenade the customers while serving mince pies. The café has reached a section of the community with which the church had lost touch and acts as a bridge between church and community.

Le Prix	
Coffee	80p
Flavoured syrup	10p
Tea	50p
Hot chocolate with cream and/or mallows	100p
Juice and biscuit	20p

The Pepperpot
Fairfield, Buxton

When The Buxton Methodist Circuit launched its Faith in Fairfield Project in 1998, supported by Methodism's Resourcing Mission Fund, it was hoped that given time it would:

- become ecumenical
- find an operational centre
- be a community resource

Three years on, The Pepperpot was born.

Café scheme after survey's food for thought

A former butcher's shop on Victoria Park Road, Fairfield, has been given a new lease of life and is now a thriving community café.

Thanks to Buxton Methodist Circuit, St Peter's Church, Fairfield, and members of the Fairfield Community Trust, the café has taken over the site between the post office and Residents of Fairfield Association.

The café has been christened The Pepperpot and is the result of a project led by churches and community organisations to provide residents in the area with what they wanted most – a base in the neighbourhood where people of all ages could meet and get a decent cup of tea.

David Harris, a lay worker from Buxton Methodist Circuit, said: 'Towards the end of last year, a number of people and groups were asked what additional activities the churches could most usefully provide in the Fairfield area. The responses were encouraging and based on that research, over the next year we set about making the idea a reality.'

The project, which has brought back into use a building empty for seven years, was funded by pooling of church funds and donations from local trusts and businesses. Its future will rely on the help of volunteers to keep it going.

Mr Harris hopes the café will become a hub of community support and friendship in Fairfield.

'Initially, we will serve tea, coffee, soft drinks, toasties, cake, crisps and biscuits, but we will gradually increase the choice and ultimately be able to use the café as a base for a whole host of community activities,' he said.

Buxton Advertiser

The survey carried out on the estate helped sharpen the focus on the direction the work should take. Church members are involved, but it is not based within a church building. (In this instance the two nearest churches – Anglican and Methodist – are on the busy A6 away from the 6-7,000 population on the Fairfield Estate). People from the houses nearby have volunteered to serve, others have been recruited from local churches and all have completed a training course. There is a valuable community spirit within the workforce and close associations with the Fairfield Residents Association and a second-hand furniture project. It is bright, friendly and informal. Many of the customers are now greeted by name. As a result, a better community identity and more positive attitude is being created within Fairfield.

Full breakfasts, a meal of the day at lunchtime, snacks to take away, are all popular. The first Pepperpot Christmas Lunches were the talk of the town.

LOCAL AND GLOBAL

In our world, the status quo no longer exists. If we should no longer use old ways to engage new realities, how do we read the signs of the times and respond to them. For it is inconceivable for a faith centred on a Christ-like God not to do so. Reading the signs of the times and responding to them will certainly involve being global in our thinking and acting. Within that global context, certain questions must be addressed, from the demands of a global economy and the challenge of demographic explosion, with implications for the environment, to growing marginalisation between and within nations. The sheer scale of these questions in an increasingly integrated world demands large responses. Religion is integrally linked to global contexts and questions as part both of the problem, as fundamentalism, and of solutions through commitments to justice, peace and loving relationships. There can therefore be no retreat from the Christian task of developing public theologies of global proportions. Without such constructive interactions we will not survive gracefully on this planet.

     – JOHN ATHERTON, *Public Theology for Changing Times*

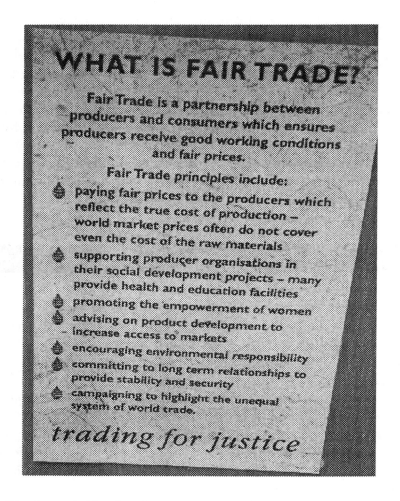

Fair Trade and Traidcraft are mentioned numerous times in the Directory, with some church cafés giving these vital links with the global economy a very high profile.

Fair Shares Café
Emmanuel United Reformed Church, Cambridge

> ## Quality fare with fair shares all round!

By choosing to eat and drink in this café a person becomes a principal partner in seeking peace and justice in all departments of life, including the realm of supply and demand. Through using Traidcraft products and cutting out profit-making 'middle-people', a fair return is offered to hardworking and hard-up Third World producers. The café is staffed by a mixture of volunteer helpers from the church and people with learning disabilities from the Edmund House Group of Homes (Cambridge Mencap). This partnership provides a safe and supervised context for fulfilling work, acquiring new skills and learning from each other. Customers at Emmanuel are helping the church to stand alongside others who can benefit from their need for food and drink, and their money. A note on the menu is helpful to staff and customers.

> *Some of our staff have learning disabilities.*
> *To ensure we fill your order correctly,*
> *please complete an order form by indicating*
> *how many of each numbered dish you*
> *require.*

The Fare Shares Café is one among many partnerships encouraged by Emmanuel's Ministry and Mission programme.

Just Connections⊞

*Imagination matters – Only as we paint pictures inside
our heads can the situation of others be understood.
Facts, figures, ideas help our heads; imagination feeds
our hearts. We need both our hearts and our heads.*

— PETER HAYWOOD

Just Connections was established by Peter, a Methodist minister, in
1980 and is a network of people across the country seeking to
enhance the causes of people across the world through a wider
perspective and right and just connections based on:

- the personal – people acting together through partners
  across the world
- making real connections – gratitude to caring, privilege to
  justice, faith to action, compassion to solidarity
- being a window to help people see the world

Over the years this vision has attracted and inspired hundreds of people, particularly young people, and involved them in numerous campaigns, overseas visits and small projects in several countries including China, Hungary, Nicaragua, Kenya and Bangladesh. Recently Just Connections facilitated a children's dining centre and clinic on the edges of Managua, the capital of Nicaragua.

Every month Just Connections gives regular, reliable financial support to:

- Send a Cow
- L'Arche Community worldwide
- Traidcraft Exchange
- Voluntary Services Overseas
- Intermediate Technology
- Ashoka UK (which funds social entrepreneurs whose insights can change societies)
- Amos Trust (operating Community Houses in the Philippines, South Africa, Palestine

166

During Peter's ministry in **Garstang**, a small market town between Preston and Lancaster, his vision of a Fairtrade Shop to promote awareness of the plight of the Third World communities struggling to overcome poverty, so motivated church members that in 1991 they converted a former youth wing at the Methodist Church into a shop. The name **Mustard Seed** was chosen by competition and it is a bustling meeting place where customers can be served with tea or coffee and admire the crafts and stationery from around the world. Contacts have been made not only with UK suppliers of Fairtrade foods and crafts, but also directly with communities in India, Indonesia, Guatemala, Nepal and Romania. Handmade products in, for example, cotton, soapstone, recycled paper and jewellery may be purchased as well as a wide selection of greetings cards.

All profits are ploughed back into buying stock and helping craftsmen and women to have a future in their homelands across four continents.

From this seed, the people of Garstang have responded to the leadership of the local Oxfam group by declaring it to be the first Fairtrade town. Shops, supermarkets, health food stores and retailers on garage forecourts are part of the Garstang Fairtrade Directory.

The Beacon at **Heswall** Methodist Church shares the same vision. It was established in 1998 in a large house owned by the church and next door to it. Twice yearly the forty volunteers who staff the Beacon meet to decide on the distribution of profits to charities at home and abroad.

These few illustrations serve to remind us of the challenge to church cafés to respond to the cry for justice echoed in this prayer:

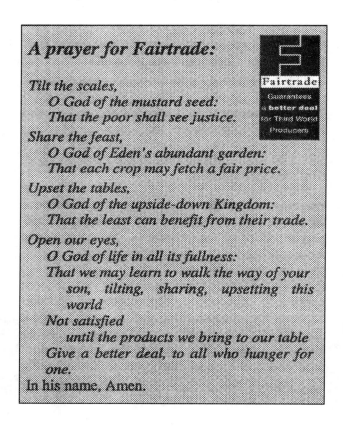

A prayer for Fairtrade:

Tilt the scales,
 O God of the mustard seed:
 That the poor shall see justice.
Share the feast,
 O God of Eden's abundant garden:
 That each crop may fetch a fair price.
Upset the tables,
 O God of the upside-down Kingdom:
 That the least can benefit from their trade.
Open our eyes,
 O God of life in all its fullness:
 That we may learn to walk the way of your
  son, tilting, sharing, upsetting this
  world
 Not satisfied
  until the products we bring to our table
 Give a better deal, to all who hunger for
 one.
In his name, Amen.

Behind the Scenes

A glance at the Directory reveals that most church cafés are sustained by the goodwill of volunteers. This is not to underestimate the contribution made by full-time or part-time paid staff appointed to ensure the smooth running of larger enterprises. Often they are supported by a rota of volunteers.

If 'willing horses' are not to be flogged there must be continual recruitment and a poster in the café or a note on the menu will make this point:

WANTED – VOLUNTEERS!
The Open House, Bath

Would you like to join our team of volunteers who help with serving at the till, or with table clearing/befriending?

If so, please contact the Manager or Assistant Manager

The list below should help clarify your thoughts;
if you would like more information or a sight of the roster,
please ask at the counter.
If you would need help with transport,
please let us know.

- **How often could you assist?**
(Once a week, twice a week, once a fortnight, occasionally, etc.)

- **Which day or days of the week?**

- **Morning or afternoon?**

THE STABLE, NEWMARKET

Voluntary Helpers work alongside our members of staff in a variety of practical ways including:
- *catering,*
- *serving our customers in the coffee bar,*
- *public relations,*
- *general help and administration,*
- *working with young people.*

We need people with a wide variety of skills who would be committed to giving us some of their precious time to help continue to develop and maintain this very valuable and much needed resource for the community.

If you are interested in becoming a voluntary helper, then please contact:

To all our Visitors at The Well

You've found a seat – quite an achievement at a busy time! – you've ordered your refreshments; so, whilst you have a few moments to spare, could we ask you to read this?

The Well is staffed by volunteers and like all such organisations, we are constantly short of staff. I'm a volunteer here and I can tell you that the job gives you an aching back, tired feet, a few bruises and wonderful companionship and a lot of laughs! I became a volunteer because I was new to living in Malvern and needed to meet people. I now have an ever-expanding group of friends who mean a lot to me.

170

They say: 'If you want something done, ask a busy person.' We're sure that is what you are; but if by any chance you could spare 3 hours a week, would you consider giving us a try? Any of the folks in 'the Upper Room' would love to talk to you whenever it suits you.

Thank you for taking the time to read this. Enjoy your meal.

The Lyttleton Well, Malvern

What is the age range of the volunteers? How far do they travel to the café? What work experience (or previous work experience) do they have? This would be an interesting exercise for any café to complete. Here is one example:

Liskeard Manna

Age range: 17–82

Travel involved: up to 8 miles

Work experience:

A-level students	Nurse/psychiatric nurse
Audiologist	Secretaries
Bank administration manager	Shopkeeper
Bookseller	Social worker
Farmer	Supernumerary Methodist
Farmers' wives	Minister
Housewives	Teachers
Jeweller	(including domestic science)
Meteorologist	YMCA worker
NCH worker	*Many are retired*

Ratio of men to women: mainly women, say 5-1.

The majority of cafés listed gave the precise number of volunteers making a total of 3,790. Taking into consideration the fact that cafés discovered may only be the tip of the iceberg, what a vast army of volunteers there must be. Spare a thought for those who compile the rotas. It must be such a relief when the next few months are covered and reserves are on call to step in at the last minute when required.

> An older woman, faithful member of a church in a deprived inner city community, regularly served tea and toast to local mothers in the church hall. It was a place to come and meet others, to relax and laugh together. A theological student on placement there sat and listened to her work and helped her to see how her service connected to the gospel stories of service, even to death on the cross. So she now saw what she was doing and why. Not that it changed what she did, but it was now so different. She had appropriated the Christian story of reconciliation in and through her partnership involvement.

> – JOHN ATHERTON, *Public Theology for Changing Times*

PASTORAL

There must be many personal stories related to cafés and numerous instances of pastoral care offered. It is important to respect confidentiality. In a book called *Living Water – The Story of the Lyttleton Well* there is a section entitled 'Drinking the Water – A Few of the Many Stories from the Well'. Permission has been given by the **Lyttleton Well** and Emily's family for one such story to be included in this book:

Emily's Story
by Alison Bennett

In November 1993 my youngest daughter, Emily, aged four, appeared unwell. It was during a 'flu outbreak, when many of our friends were suffering similar symptoms. As she didn't seem to be picking up I took her to our Doctor's. On the second visit he seemed concerned, and suggested that we took her to our County Hospital right away. An hour or two on we stood beside the Consultant staring in disbelief at a picture of a huge tumour on a scan of Emily's brain. Our world fell apart.

Three days later Emily had major brain surgery at the Children's Hospital, where the large majority of the tumour was removed. She was then ventilated on the Intensive Care Unit and stayed in hospital a further two weeks to recuperate. We were told the tumour was malignant (cancer), and that even with further treatment it was likely to regrow within a year or so.

The day after we came out of hospital, still in a state of shock and reeling between Christian hope and human despair, I made my way into the Lyttelton Well Bookshop, looking for a book that would give me light and insight into our situation. I wanted a magic book that would answer the unformulated questions that crowded my mind. I asked the assistant for help in selecting a book and he introduced me to Richard, the Manager. I hadn't gone for sympathy and support, but found myself pouring out the details of our situation. Richard promised that the centre would pray for us in their daily prayer time. He kept in touch with us by phone and came across to meet us in our church one Sunday morning.

Emily went through an intensive course of radiotherapy and in time she gained strength again so that she was able to start school the following Easter. We tried to regain normal family life and not to focus on her cancer. We could do this until the time would arrive for Emily's six-monthly scans and check ups. They would force us to refocus on the cancer and it was a scary time finding out if the tumour was regrowing or not. I would let Richard know as the appointment time arrived and the Lyttelton Well would join our friends in surrounding us with prayer.

Two and a half years on from her diagnosis, Emily relapsed.

This time we chose not to put Emily through further treatment and we took her home to love her to her death. Not that Emily minded the fact that she would die. She would 'see Jesus, see his real face' (her words). The day Emily left us for heaven, Richard joined us with a couple of friends to pray with us. He also led a time of prayer for us the following Sunday evening at our church.

Christian or not, losing a child is agony and Emily's death left a deep chasm of pain in our life. As I tried to support our other two children in their grief, I found it helpful to speak to a counsellor at the Well, and to use her as a sounding board. A year on, Richard sensitively led our own little service of Remembrance for Emily, with our closest friends present. He had composed the most beautiful song, based on Emily's words.

Scripture tells us to carry one another's burdens. The Lyttelton Well joined with those other faithful band of God's people and enabled us to feel very loved and very accompanied. God embraced us through those most painful of times through the love-in-action of his people. Thank you, Lord, for not leaving us alone.

And from Liskeard Manna ...

To my dearest friends I met at the coffee shop and who gave me aid at my lowest times in my bad spell. Now life has taken a U-turn and I am now in a very happy home and with very good benefit situations after almost twelve months. I thank all for your help and support. Never will I forget a little coffee shop who were my only access to warmth and much more.

May your God bless you.
My love, 'Foxxy' (Punk)

(message from a Greetings Card received and quoted with permission)

These two illustrations give just a glimpse of pastoral opportunities presented when doors are open. Who knows who will walk in and with what needs or questions. Church cafés are an Open Invitation, not merely to sample the menu, but to unburden and to ask relevant questions. Listening is very important and has been mentioned many times in this book. Our ev*angel*ism needs to cherish the *angel* in the middle. Henry Burton's lines in the hymn, 'There's a light upon the mountains ...' remind us that God's ministering angels in this world are people:

> But his Angels here are human,
> Not the shining hosts above;
> For the drum-beats of his army
> Are the heart-beats of our love.

Some conversations may lead naturally in the direction of a book or booklet that will help. The sharing of appropriate literature between cafés could form part of the networking, possibly stimulated by this book.

On **The Open Door** menu at **Hampton Magna, Warwick,** the desire to minister to the whole person is expressed in a few lines:

We hope you will find that The Open Door is:

In your body –
Refreshing you with
Fairly traded drinks & snacks

In your mind –
Informing you of local
And world issues from a
Christian perspective

In your heart –
Bringing you the
Opportunity to grow spiritually.

In Romans chapter 12 St Paul speaks of the gifts of God present within the Christian community and the way in which those scattered gifts can be harnessed and used. Thankfully he mentions the gift of administration, suggesting that order is to be preferred to chaos.

Behind every cup of tea or coffee, toasted teacake or three-course meal there is a plethora of administration. In preparing for their new venture at **Wesley's** in **Harpenden**, the Project Planning Group Committee took seriously St Paul's words and designated six priorities to be co-ordinated.

Catering Co-ordinator

Key Contributions
- To assist in selecting an appropriate range of refreshments.
- To ensure Environmental Health regulations are met.
- To oversee purchasing and stock control.

Key Qualities and Experience
- An understanding of Environmental Health issues.
- A willingness to be innovative where appropriate.
- Ability to liaise well with other team members and customers.

Finance Co-ordinator

Key Contributions
- To ensure monies are transferred to church safe at end of each session, and banked weekly.
- To keep accounts and ensure these are audited and available to the church treasurer.
- To liaise with staff and Management Team to select charities to be supported by proceeds (including donations to church funds and to continuing Opening Doors funds).
- To monitor budgets (including catering; maintenance of furnishings and equipment; publicity).

- To liaise with church treasurer to ensure appropriate contributions are made for caretaking, utilities, insurance etc.

Key Qualities and Experience
- Good accounting skills.
- Ability to liaise with other people.

Maintenance Co-ordinator

Key Contributions
- Ensure room and equipment are kept clean and tidy.
- Ensure equipment is properly maintained.
- Liaise with service and repair engineers.
- Advise on servicing contracts.
- Carry out repairs / arrange for repairs to be carried out.

Key Qualities and Experience
- A conscientious approach and practical skills.
- Ability to liaise well with other church users.

Prayer and Resources Co-ordinator

Key contributions
- To motivate people to pray for all aspects of Wesley's.
- To find ways to fulfil the Christian potential of the project.
- To pray specifically for the staff and visitors to Wesley's.
- To promote the loan / sale / free-giving of Christian books etc.
- To ensure church events etc. are appropriately promoted within Wesley's.

Key Qualities and Experience
- A heart and imagination for prayer.
- Good communication skills to motivate others to pray.

Publicity Co-ordinator

Key Contributions
- To promote Wesley's in the church and community.
- To liaise with Church Outreach team in developing a range of events which could take place in the venue.
- To advertise particular events.

Key Qualities and Experience
- A strong desire to fulfil the outreach potential.
- Communication skills – both oral and written.

Staff Co-ordinator
Key Contributions
- Recruit staff to serve refreshments.
- Arrange appropriate training.
- Prepare rota (e.g. 6 months at a time) plus list of reserve helpers.
- Be prepared to fill rota gaps at short notice where possible.
- Liaise with other members of Wesley's team, including Saturday and Sunday helpers.

Key Qualities and Experience
- Good at communicating.
- Encouraging.

At **All Saints, Leighton Buzzard,** every effort has been made to ensure good practice.

NOTES FOR COFFEE SHOP HELPERS

Aims of the coffee shop

To be the servant of the Church by providing:
1. *A pleasant, friendly place for visitors to the church to have light refreshments.*
2. *An informal meeting place for church members and friends.*
3. *A service to the wider Community and a possible 'Way In' to church for our customers.*
4. *A means of income to the church.*

A few points of general procedure & policy of the coffee shop

1. *We aim to provide a pleasant surrounding for our customers, hence the need for cleanliness, tidiness, flowers, pictures and a lack of church clutter and notices. We want all visitors to feel comfortable and not as if they are venturing into a church meeting room.*

2. *We provide a very few up-to-date magazines to encourage people, especially those on their own, to stay. We try to discourage gifts of old magazines!*

3. *We stress the importance of the attitude of the helpers in creating the right atmosphere, i.e. friendly and welcoming. We make a point of greeting people when they come in and saying Goodbye when they leave. We try to speak to everyone during their visit, remembering that it is more important to chat to customers than to our fellow helpers.*

4. *We try particularly to be sensitive to visitors. The seating area is small, and can very easily seem like a church club, which can in turn make visitors feel excluded. We try to be aware of this situation and remedy it, by including visitors in the conversation. However, some people may come in for peace and quiet. It is important to try and spot this and not be to pressing if our attempts at conversation are obviously not welcomed.*

5. *We are occasionally visited by tramps. We supply a drink free of charge if requested.*

6. *Accident and emergency routine. There is a First Aid Kit by the handwashing sink for coping with minor accidents. In the event of any serious accident or emergency, use the telephone in the office to summon assistance or call the Administrator for extra help. There is a fire extinguisher and fire blanket for kitchen use, but only deal with fires yourself if safe to do so. In all but the smallest fire evacuate the premises at once. The fire alarm is connected to the Fire Station.*

7. *There is a personal alarm under the counter, which should be used if helpers feel threatened in any way.*

We didn't know ...

Charities, or other community groups, taking over a café on an occasional basis, need to follow careful instructions so that they can never say, 'We didn't know.' At **St Nicholas Centre in Whitehaven** they can't go wrong if the careful instructions provided are followed:

It is important that you confirm your booking four weeks before the date otherwise you may lose your day

Please take away all your boxes

- TURN ON IMMERSION HEATER
  Switch behind dish washer
- MAKE COFFEE
  Follow instructions kept left of machine
- BOIL EGGS AND MILK
- SET UP COUNTER
  Cruets on tables
- PREPARE SANDWICH FILLINGS
- PREPARE SANDWICHES
  Salad popular
- TOASTIES
  Margarine to outside – NOT GOLD
  Toast at 4 – DO NOT leave toaster empty

FOOD SUPPLIED
- All drinks
- Milk
- Biscuits
- Margarine (Gold)
- Sandwich filling (except meat)
- Soup (unless otherwise stated)

YOU TO SUPPLY
- Bread (medium sliced)

- Ham
- Scones
- Cakes
- Sausage Rolls
- Own tea towels and float

Approx. quantity
4 wholemeal
3 white
15 slices
4–5 dozen
6 dozen portions
18

DO NOT FORGET OWN FLOAT FOR CAFÉ, CAKES, TEA TOWELS, RAFFLE

LIGHT SWITCHES
- Left of Stairs
- Porch – Right of front door

Leave 25% of kitchen takings in safe,
together with the total figure raised in kitchen and shop

END OF DAY
- Put out rubbish (wheelie bin at back)
- Switch off immersion heater
- Empty and rinse coffee jugs
- Switch off and unplug machine

Seen in a café:

WILL LADIES PLEASE RINSE OUT TEAPOTS
THEN STAND UPSIDE-DOWN IN THE SINK.

ON NO ACCOUNT
MUST HOT BOTTOMS BE PLACED ON THE
WORK-TOPS

At **Manvers Street** in **Bath** the table mats are plastic wallets containing information about church activities for the month:

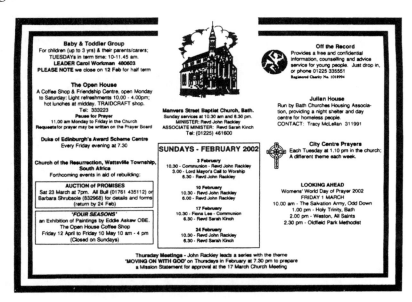

Baby & Toddler Group
For children (up to 3 yrs) & their parents/carers;
TUESDAYs in term time: 10-11.45 am.
LEADER Carol Workman 480603
PLEASE NOTE we close on 12 Feb for half term

The Open House
A Coffee Shop & Friendship Centre, open Monday
to Saturday: Light refreshments 10.00 - 4.00pm;
hot lunches at midday. TRAIDCRAFT shop.
Tel: 333223
Pause for Prayer
11.00 am Monday to Friday in the Church
Requests for prayer may be written on the Prayer Board

Duke of Edinburgh's Award Scheme Centre
Every Friday evening at 7.30

**Church of the Resurrection, Wattsville Township,
South Africa**
Forthcoming events in aid of rebuilding:

AUCTION of PROMISES
Sat 23 March at 7pm. All Bull (01761 435112) or
Barbara Shrubsole (832968) for details and forms
(return by 24 Feb)

'FOUR SEASONS'
an Exhibition of Paintings by Eddie Askew OBE.
The Open House Coffee Shop
Friday 12 April to Friday 10 May 10 am - 4 pm
(Closed on Sundays)

Manvers Street Baptist Church, Bath.
Sunday services at 10.30 am and 6.30 pm.
MINISTER: Revd John Rackley
ASSOCIATE MINISTER: Revd Sarah Kinch
Tel: (01225) 461600

SUNDAYS - FEBRUARY 2002

3 February
10.30 - Communion - Revd John Rackley
3.00 - Lord Mayor's Call to Worship
6.30 - Revd John Rackley

10 February
10.30 - Revd John Rackley
6.00 - Revd John Rackley

17 February
10.30 - Fiona Lee - Communion
6.30 - Revd Sarah Kinch

24 February
10.30 - Revd John Rackley
6.30 - Revd Sarah Kinch

Thursday Meetings - John Rackley leads a series with the theme
'MOVING ON WITH GOD' on Thursdays in February at 7.30 pm to prepare
a Mission Statement for approval at the 17 March Church Meeting

Off the Record
Provides a free and confidential
information, counselling and advice
service for young people. Just drop in,
or phone 01225 335551
Registered Charity No. 1018994

Julian House
Run by Bath Churches Housing Association, providing a night shelter and day
centre for homeless people.
CONTACT: Tracy McLellan 311991

City Centre Prayers
Each Tuesday at 1.10 pm in the church;
A different theme each week.

LOOKING AHEAD
Womens' World Day of Prayer 2002
FRIDAY 1 MARCH
10.00 am - The Salvation Army, Odd Down
1.00 pm - Holy Trinity, Bath
2.00 pm - Weston, All Saints
2.30 pm - Oldfield Park Methodist

MANVERS STREET DURING FEBRUARY 2002 - Dates for Your Diary

		3	10	17	24
SUN	February	10.30 - Revd John Rackley -Communion. 3.00 - Lord Mayor's call to worship 6.30 - Revd John Rackley. FLOWERS In loving memory of Jack (Dad & Pops) who left us such lovely memories - Elsie, Susan & Zella and the American Reids	10.30 - Revd John Rackley 6.00 - Revd John Rackley. FLOWERS Margaret Wake	10.30 - Fiona Lee - Communion 6.30 - Revd Sarah Kinch (Holy Places, Sacred Spaces). FLOWERS Frank and Pat North	10.30 -Revd John Rackley 6.30 - Revd Sarah Kinch (Holy Places, Sacred Spaces). FLOWERS Gwen Heamshaw in loving memory of her parents
		4	11	18	25
MON					
		5	12	19	26
TUE		10.00 Baby & Toddler Group 1.10 City Centre Prayers. 6.30 - Healing Service, Uni Chaplaincy	1.10 City Centre Prayers 7.30 Deacons Meeting	10.00 Baby & Toddler Group 1.10 City Centre Prayers. 6.30 - Healing Service, Uni Chaplaincy	10.00 Baby & Toddler Group 1.10 City Centre Prayers 7.30 Church Meeting
		6	13	20	27
WED		1.00 Julian Meeting, Holy Trinity 2.30 WOMENS' FELLOWSHIP - Mr P. Baxterfield - American Birds (Blue)	2.30 WOMENS' FELLOWSHIP - Revd Sarah Kinch	2.30 WOMENS' FELLOWSHIP - Mr Bob Porton - Radio Comedy. 6.00 Julian Prayer meeting, Holy Trinity	2.30 WOMENS' FELLOWSHIP - T.O. Choir
		7	14	21	28
THU		10.00 - Thursday People. 7.30 - 'Moving on with God'	10.00 - Thursday People. 7.30 - 'Moving on with God'. CHURCH NEWS DEADLINE	10.00 - Thursday People. 7.30 - 'Moving on with God'	10.00 - Thursday People. 7.30 - 'Moving on with God'
FRI	7.45 - John Rackley, Radio Bristol **1** 7.30 Duke of Edinburgh's Award Scheme	7.45 - John Rackley, Radio Bristol **8** 7.30 Duke of Edinburgh's Award	7.45 - John Rackley, Radio Bristol **15** 7.30 Duke of Edinburgh's Award	7.45 - John Rackley, Radio Bristol **22** 7.30 Duke of Edinburgh's Award	
SAT	**2**	**9**	**16**	**23**	

(The OPEN HOUSE COFFEE SHOP is open Monday to Saturday 10.00. - 4.00)

What's on offer?

Some cafés design attractive menu folders and boards:

SANDWICH MENU

Please ask if you do not see it - we may just have some!
Take a look at our specials board for great new tastes.

	Large Bap	Sandwich	French Stick/ Torpedo
Egg Mayo/Egg	£1.35	£1.55	£1.95
Cheese (with pickle if desired) [V]	£1.35	£1.55	£1.95
Cheese and Coleslaw [V]	£1.35	£1.55	£1.95
Cottage Cheese [V]	£1.35	£1.55	£1.95
Tuna Mayonaisse	£1.35	£1.55	£1.95
Cumberland Sausage and Stuffing	£1.65	£1.85	£2.45
(hot or cold)	£1.65	£1.85	£2.45
Brie and Apple [V]	£1.65	£1.85	£2.45
Bacon, Lettuce and Tomato	£1.65	£1.85	£2.45
(hor or cold)	£1.65	£1.85	£2.45
Ham, Pork, Chicken or Turkey	£1.65	£1.85	£2.45
(subject to availability)	£1.65	£1.85	£2.45
Houmous and Tomato [V]	£1.65	£1.85	£2.45
Ham, Cream Cheese and Pineapple	£1.85	£2.05	£2.95
Chicken Tikka	£1.85	£2.05	£2.95
Coronation Chicken	£1.85	£2.05	£2.95
Pork, Apple and Stuffing	£1.85	£2.05	£2.95
Beef and Horseradish	£1.85	£2.05	£2.95
World famous dubré!!	£1.85	£2.05	£2.95
(Bacon, Mushroom and Cheese)	£1.85	£2.05	£2.95
Specials from the board	£1.85	£2.05	£2.95

[V] = Suitable for Vegetarians

Side salad at no extra charge on the above

All the above are available in white or brown bread except the French sticks and torpedos

Service at your discretion

(Andover)

GAP - A THANET COMMUNITY PROJECT

Café Gap
part of the GAP project

Tel: 01843 861055
e-mail - gapcharity.fsnet.co.uk
Charity No: 1084622

Opening times 10.30 'til 1.30

Served from 11.30 'til 1.30

Soup of the Day
Served with soft roll and butter   £1

Create a meal from any of the choices below
Main Meals Cooked to Order.
Burger in a bun	50p
Chips	45p
* Burger Beef	35p
* Burger Minted Lamb	35p
Bacon	30p
* Sausage	30p
Ham	30p
Soft Roll	15p
Egg	15p
Beans	15p
Peas	15p

Jacket Potatoes
Whole Potato	£1.20
choice of the following fillings	
Cottage Cheese	30p
Cheese	30p
Tuna	30p
Beans	15p
Pineapple	10p

or any of the above in Main Meals section

* Freshly Made by a Local Butcher

Served from 10.30

Cakes and Desserts
Cheesecake	60p
Cakes and slices	50p
Fresh Cream Trifle	60p

Drinks
Tea	40p
Bottomless cup of tea	70p
Coffee	50p
Bottomless cup of coffee	80p
Cola or Fruit Crush	30p
Fresh Orange Juice	30p
Black Currant Squash	10p
Orange Squash	10p

Check the notice board to see if there is a special on to day

(Broadstairs)

184

Community Café Menu

Healthy Eating At Affordable Prices

Drinks	Cup	Mug
♥ Coffee	35	45
♥ Tea	30	40
Hot Chocolate		45
Hot Chocolate with cream		55

By the Glass	
♥ Cordial	30
♥ Fresh Orange	40
♥ Milk	40
♥ Milk Shake	50

Cakes and Desserts
As individually Priced
With Custard or Cream 20p extra

Hot Meals from £1.50
For today's Specials see the Notice Board

♥ are Healthy Options

Buffet & Catering Service
available from
The Community Café.
Please contact:
Maggie Carrington
or **Sharon Murrey** at:

The Geoffrey Allen
Church and County Centre
Winster Mews
Gamesley
GLOSSOP
Derbyshire
SK13 0LU

Jacket Potatoes
with these fillings

♥ Tuna	1.40	♥ Beans	1.20
Cheese	1.30	Butter	90
Cheese + Beans	1.50		

Cold Sandwiches
on a brown or white muffin

♥ Beef	80	♥ Tuna Mayonnaise	90
♥ Ham	80	Cheese	80
♥ Salad	60	Cheese + Ham	1.00
♥ Turkey	80		

Cold Sandwich Extras

♥ Salad	20	♥ Lettuce	10
♥ Tomatoes	10	♥ Cucumber	10
♥ Pickle	10	♥ Beetroot	10
Cheese	20	♥ Onion	10

Pies

Meat + Potato	95
Steak	1.10
Pasties	95

Set Breakfast
Special price £2.10

Bacon, Sausage, Mushrooms, Egg, Toast
Beans/Tomatoes + Mug of Tea or Coffee

All other breakfasts charged at individual prices

♥ are Healthy Options

Eat More Fruit & Veg

Hot Sandwiches
on a white or brown muffin or toast

Cheese + Onion	1.00
Bacon	1.20
Sausage	1.20
Sausage + Bacon	1.40
B.L.T.	1.40
Hot roast beef, onion + gravy	1.40
Cheese	90
Eggs on toast	90
♥ Beans on toast	90
♥ Scrambled Egg on Toast	90

Hot Sandwich Extras

♥ Beans	20	Cheese	20
Egg	25	♥ Tinned tomatoes	30
Fried tomatoes	20	Fried onions	25
Mushrooms	30		

Omelettes

♥ Plain	1.00
Cheese	1.20
♥ Mushroom	1.35
Salad 20p extra	

Breakfast Items

Bacon	50	Sausage	35
♥ Beans	25	Eggs	25
Tomatoes	25	Toast	20
Mushrooms	35	Fried Toms	35
Fried Onions	35	♥ Scrambled Egg	50

Be Kind to Your Heart

Eat Less Fat

(Glossop)

185

Kathy's Survey in Old Basing

So, how was it for you ?

I am a mum with three children at school in Old Basing and I am doing a course, training to be a priest. As part of my course I have to do some research into my local community. I would like to look at the experience of being a mum.
 I would be really grateful if you could fill in one of these questionnaires and return it to school via your child before March 31st. I have included an envelope so that your reply will be anonymous.
Many thanks

Kathy O'Loughlin

Are you in paid employment? Yes/No   Full time?   Part time?

Does being a mum live up to the expectations you had before you had children?
Yes?   In what way?

No?   In what way?

How have your expectations changed?

Do you feel that being a mum has changed you?
If so how?

What do mums of school age children need?

Do they get it?!

Do you feel that the Church can play any part in meeting these needs?

how/why?

Those who use 'Hartley's' may be interested to know that it links them with a prominent Methodist, Sir William Pickles Hartley (1846–1922). He was knighted in 1908.

Hartley became a jam manufacturer by accident. A local supplier failed to honour a contract to supply Hartley's Colne grocer's shop with jam. Hartley therefore decided to make jam himself. The popularity of this home-made product caused Hartley to abandon his grocery business and concentrate on jam manufacture. In 1874 he built a factory in Palm Grove, Bootle and later moved to Aintree, Liverpool. A London factory at Tower Bridge Road was also established in 1901. Hartley had been brought up a Primitive Methodist and, for a time, was organist at the Colne Primitive Methodist Church. His Nonconformist conscience impelled him to care for his employees and practise stewardship with regard to wealth. On 1 January 1877 Mr and Mrs Hartley made a written vow to 'devote a definite and well considered share of their income for religious and humanitarian work.' This, Hartley conceived to be one of the best checks to that natural selfishness which is inherent in human nature.

(A. S. Peake, *The Life of Sir William Hartley* published in 1926 by Hodder and Stoughton and quoted by Dr Kenneth Lysons in *A Little Primitive – Primitive Methodism from Macro and Micro Perspectives* published in 2001 by Church in the Market Place Publications, Buxton.)

Where are they?

You could easily mistake them for church cafés:

Spirit Café

The first correct entry will receive a free copy of this book.

Cafés Continued

These late entries give a start to listing cafés discovered by readers of this book.

BLACKHEATH

Central Methodist Church
High Street
Blackheath
WESLEY'S
West Midlands

Open: Monday, Tuesday, Thursday and Saturday 9.30 a.m. to 12 noon
Staff: 9 volunteers
Menu: Tea, coffee, biscuits and snacks, toast. Tuesday and Thursday breakfasts are served.

Started in June 2002.

KNUTSFORD

147 Longridge
Knutsford
WELCOME CAFÉ
WA16 8PD

Open: Monday to Friday 10.00 a.m. to 3 p.m.

WELCOME CAFÉ CHURCH
Open: Sundays 2.30 p.m.

This is the coming together of people from the local estate, many unchurched, as a community exploring and finding faith in Jesus Christ. It meets every Sunday for a time of worship, teaching, prayer and fellowship. However, Café Church is not just on a Sunday, but is all that happens during the week, expressing itself in the many areas that we are involved in within the community.

PERTH

The North Church
Mill Street
Perth

THE OPEN DOOR

Open: Monday to Friday 2 p.m. to 4 p.m.
Staff: 25 volunteers.

Started in 1997.